easy barbecue

easy barbecue

simply delicious recipes for outdoor cooking

RYLAND
PETERS
& SMALL

LONDON NEW YORK

Senior Designer Toni Kay
Editor Rebecca Woods
Picture Research Emily Westlake
Production Toby Marshall
Art Director Leslie Harrington
Publishing Director Alison Starling

Indexer Hilary Bird

First published in the United Kingdom
in 2011 by Ryland Peters & Small
20–21 Jockey's Fields
London WC1R 4BW
www.rylandpeters.com

10 9 8 7 6 5 4 3 2

Text © Ghillie Başan, Fiona Beckett, Maxine
Clark, Ross Dobson, Jane Noraika, Louise
Pickford, Fiona Smith, Lindy Wildsmith and
Ryland Peters & Small 2011

Design and commissioned photographs
© Ryland Peters & Small 2011

ISBN: 978-1-84975-110-0

A CIP record for this book is available from
the British Library.

Printed and bound in China

contents

introduction

Barbecues are one of the best ways to make the most of a warm summer's day. Adaptable to any occasion – from an impromptu meal for two on a city balcony, to a large party in a country garden – barbecues are so versatile and always seem to inject a sense of adventure into cooking. Whether you choose a gas barbecue, for the convenience of being able to spark up as soon as the clouds part, or are wedded to the delicious smoky taste delivered by a charcoal grill, barbecuing has become one of our favourite methods of cooking and entertaining.

In celebration of outdoor cooking, *Easy Barbecue* is full of recipes which are simple to prepare, often in advance, so that you can relax and enjoy the al fresco setting and the company. Along with barbecue classics, such as cheeseburgers and chicken wings, are recipes inspired from around the world. From Chicken Kebabs Moroccan-style, to Vietnamese Pork Balls, Sicilian-spiced Sea Bass to Mexican-style Poussins, there is something here to excite every taste bud. But if those don't tempt, turn straight to the Sauces, Marinades & Dips chapter and create your own flavour sensations.

What many people don't realize is that barbecues are not only for your burgers and sausages. Vegetables are also delicious when prepared over coals and so *Easy Barbecue* includes lots of great ideas for exciting vegetable sides and original vegetarian options. With suggestions for barbecue-baked desserts and delicious drinks too, this collection of recipes will inspire you to create a mouthwatering barbecued feast, full of the aromas of summer.

barbecue basics

While cooking on a barbecue is much simpler than you may imagine, there are a few things to remember before you start cooking. Follow the guidelines below for handy hints on choosing and making the most of your barbecue, and essential tips on fire and food safety, to keep everyone safe and happy.

Choosing a barbecue

Barbecues come in all shapes, sizes, varieties and prices from small disposable aluminium grills sold in supermarkets or hardware stores to the larger and often hugely expensive covered grills. Some barbecues have both a grill and a flat plate offering versatility, but this is not essential. The recipes will work on any of the following.

Purists would probably argue for charcoal to fuel their barbecues, but many people prefer and find it easier to opt for gas or electric ones. It is certainly debatable as to what will give the best flavour to the food but it comes down to personal choice.

For a charcoal barbecue you can use either standard briquettes or hardwood lump charcoal. The former may contain chemicals from the process used to make it, which although totally safe may effect the flavour of the food cooked over it. Hardwood lump charcoal is not as readily available as the briquettes but contains no additives, burns easily,

gets far hotter and lasts longer.

Portable barbecues are essential if you want to cook away from home (unless your chosen site has permanent barbecues) and these too come in a wide selection of styles. Again be aware of weight, the lighter the better, someone has to carry it. Portable barbecues can be either charcoal or gas, but remember coals stay hot for sometime so you must find somewhere you can legally and safely leave them or wait until they are totally cold before carefully packing them in a bag to take with you.

Safety is extremely important in barbecuing, especially if you are in parkland as many places will be a fire risk. Be sensible and set the barbecue up away from dry timber or grass and always take a fire blanket or if possible a small portable fire extinguisher with you.

Cooking on a charcoal barbecue

Arrange the fuel in as large an area as your barbecue will allow, at least

10 cm deep and leaving a little room around the edges. Place a few barbecue lighters in amongst the coals and light these using a taper or matches – these will help to get the fire started. Once the coals are burning leave for about 40–45 minutes until all the flames have subsided and the coals are covered in grey ash. Hold your hand about 12 cm above the fire and count how long it can stay there. A hot fire will be only a couple of seconds a medium hot fire three to four seconds and a cool fire five to six seconds.

You can also determine the temperature for cooking by the height of the grill over the coals. Most charcoal barbecues have several rungs to set the grill, the closest to the heat being the hottest and the furthest away, the coolest.

Cleaning is best done after you have finished cooking but whilst the barbecue is still assembled so that any residual bits of food stuck to the grill can be brushed off into the

fire. Do not clean the grill with soap or water, just scrub well with a wire brush (see equipment below).

Cooking on a gas or electric barbecue

Gas and electric barbecues can be adjusted in the same way as a domestic cooker, by turning the temperature up or down. They often come with a hood enabling you to cover the food as it grills, which produces a similar effect to roasting. Alternatively, leave the lid off and grill as normal.

It is important to preheat a gas or electric barbecue until it is really hot before adding the food and then reduce the heat as necessary. This will enable the food to brown quickly on the outside sealing in the flavour in the same way as a more traditional charcoal grill will.

Cleaning is also done in the same way as for the charcoal barbecue, although you can buy special cleaners from hardware stores. For best results, follow the instructions on the back of individual products.

Equipment

Long handled tongs are essential so that you can easily turn over any foods you are cooking without allowing your hands to get too close to the heat where they can get scorched. Do not leave the tongs

on or near the heat as they too can get very hot.

Skewers can be either bamboo or metal. Bamboo skewers are disposable and will need to be pre-soaked before use, which prevents them from burning over a high heat. Metal skewers are readily available from hardware stores but remember they can get very hot, so turn them using either a tea towel or the tongs.

A sturdy wire brush is the best method for cleaning and removing bits of stuck on foods from the surface of the grill or flat plate. Give the grill a good scrub all over each time you have finished cooking and rub the flat plate with a little oil to season it each time.

Food preparation and safety

Get all the preparation done in advance – the day, the morning or an hour or two before you eat. Marinating times in the recipes are flexible, so do what suits you. Salsas, relishes, dressings and salads can be made in advance, but green salads should be dressed at the last minute. Once prepared, cover the food and refrigerate or store it in a cool place until you are ready to cook or serve it.

Most of the foods cooked on the barbecue will have started off raw. Although they must be stored in the refrigerator, it is best to return them

to room temperature for about an hour before cooking. Always keep food covered with clingfilm or a clean tea towel while they are waiting to be cooked to keep off the bugs. Once it has reached room temperature, food should be cooked as quickly as possible to prevent it from spoiling.

Once the coals are ready, arrange the meat on the grill and give it time to brown before turning. Once the meat has browned, turn it frequently and move it around the barbecue to ensure even cooking. You may need to raise the grill height if the cooking is too fast, or lower it so that it is nearer the coals if it is too slow. To lower the heat, dampen the coals slightly or close the air vent.

Make sure you cook chicken, burgers and pork thoroughly. They should be piping hot all the way through, none of the meat should be pink and the juices should run clear. Cut into meat to make sure it is cooked thoroughly. One of the major causes of food poisoning is cross contamination, so it is essential to keep raw and cooked food apart. When transferring cooked meats, fish or poultry from the grill, make sure to use clean utensils and place them on a clean cutting board or platter, not back in the unwashed dish you used to transport them to the grill.

sauces, marinades
& dips

Thai spice marinade

2 lemongrass stalks

6 kaffir lime leaves

2 garlic cloves, coarsely chopped

2 cm fresh ginger, peeled and coarsely chopped

4 coriander roots, washed and dried

2 small fresh red chillies, deseeded and coarsely chopped

200 ml extra virgin olive oil

2 tablespoons sesame oil

2 tablespoons Thai fish sauce

MAKES ABOUT 300 ML

Using a sharp knife, trim the lemongrass stalks to 15 cm, then remove and discard the tough outer layers. Chop the inner stalk coarsely.

Put the lemongrass stalks, lime leaves, garlic, ginger, coriander roots and chillies into a mortar and pound with a pestle to release the aromas.

Put the mixture into a bowl, add the oils and fish sauce and set aside to infuse until ready to use.

minted yoghurt marinade

2 teaspoons coriander seeds

1 teaspoon cumin seeds

250 ml thick yoghurt

freshly squeezed juice of ½ lemon

1 tablespoon extra virgin olive oil

2 garlic cloves, crushed

1 teaspoon grated fresh ginger

½ teaspoon sea salt

2 tablespoons chopped fresh mint

¼ teaspoon chilli powder

MAKES ABOUT 275 ML

Put the spices into a dry frying pan and toast over medium heat until golden and aromatic. Remove from the heat and let cool. Transfer to a spice grinder (or clean coffee grinder) and crush to a coarse powder. Alternatively, use a mortar and pestle.

Put the spices into a bowl, add the yoghurt, lemon juice, olive oil, garlic, ginger, salt, mint and chilli powder and mix well. Set aside to infuse until ready to use.

herb, lemon and garlic marinade

2 sprigs of fresh rosemary

2 sprigs of fresh thyme

pared zest of 1 unwaxed lemon

4 bay leaves

2 garlic cloves, coarsely chopped

1 teaspoon black peppercorns, coarsely crushed

200 ml extra virgin olive oil

MAKES ABOUT 300 ML

Strip the rosemary and thyme leaves from the stalk and put into a mortar. Add the lemon zest, bay leaves, and garlic and pound with a pestle to release the aromas.

Put the mixture into a bowl and add the crushed peppercorns and olive oil. Set aside to infuse until ready to use.

Creole rub

½ small onion, finely chopped

1 garlic clove, finely chopped

1 tablespoon chopped fresh thyme

1 tablespoon paprika

1 teaspoon ground cumin

¼ teaspoon cayenne pepper

1 tablespoon brown sugar

1 teaspoon sea salt

a little freshly ground black pepper

MAKES ABOUT 6 TABLESPOONS

Put all the ingredients into a small bowl, stir well and set aside to infuse until ready to use.

Moroccan rub

1 tablespoon coriander seeds

1 teaspoon cumin seeds

2 cinnamon sticks

1 teaspoon whole allspice berries

6 cloves

a pinch of saffron threads

1 teaspoon ground turmeric

2 teaspoons dried onion flakes

½ teaspoon paprika

1 teaspoon sea salt

MAKES ABOUT 6 TABLESPOONS

Put the whole spices and saffron threads into a dry frying pan and toast over medium heat for about 1–2 minutes or until golden and aromatic. Let cool then transfer to a spice grinder (or clean coffee grinder) and crush to a coarse powder. Alternatively, use a mortar and pestle.

Put the spices into a bowl, add the remaining ingredients and mix well. Set aside to infuse until ready to use.

fragrant Asian rub

4 whole star anise

2 teaspoons Szechuan peppercorns

1 teaspoon fennel seeds

2 small pieces of cassia bark or 1 cinnamon stick, broken

6 cloves

2 garlic cloves, finely chopped

grated zest of 2 unwaxed limes

1 teaspoon sea salt

MAKES ABOUT 6 TABLESPOONS

Put the whole spices into a dry frying pan and toast over medium heat for 1–2 minutes or until golden and aromatic. Remove from the heat and let cool. Transfer to a spice grinder (or clean coffee grinder) and crush to a coarse powder. Alternatively, use a mortar and pestle.

Put the spices into a bowl, add the garlic, lime zest and salt and mix well. Set aside to infuse until ready to use.

corn and pepper salsa

2 large corn cobs

3 tablespoons sunflower oil

4 spring onions, trimmed and thinly sliced

freshly squeezed juice of 1 lime

6 Pepperdew peppers, finely chopped

2 tablespoons finely chopped fresh coriander leaves

a dash of chilli sauce or a large pinch of mild chilli powder (optional)

sea salt and freshly ground black pepper

SERVES 4

Holding the corn cobs upright, cut down the sides with a sharp knife to remove the kernels. Heat a large frying pan over medium heat and add 2 teaspoons of the oil. Stir-fry the corn for 2–3 minutes until it begins to brown. Add the spring onions and stir-fry for 1 minute. Transfer to a bowl and let cool for 10 minutes.

Add the lime juice, peppers, coriander and the remaining oil, and mix well. Add a dash of chilli sauce, if using, and season with salt and pepper.

salsa verde

4 rounded tablespoons finely chopped fresh flat leaf parsley

1 rounded tablespoon finely chopped fresh mint leaves

2 rounded tablespoons finely chopped fresh basil leaves

100 ml extra virgin olive oil

3 spring onions, trimmed and finely chopped

2 garlic cloves, very finely chopped

2 tablespoons capers, rinsed and finely chopped

2 tablespoons gherkins, rinsed and finely chopped

3 anchovy fillets, finely chopped

2 teaspoons Dijon mustard mixed with 2 tablespoons red wine vinegar

freshly ground black pepper

SERVES 4–6

Put the herbs in a bowl with half the olive oil. Stir, add the spring onions, garlic, capers, gherkins and anchovy fillets and mix well. Add the mustard and vinegar mixture, then add enough of the remaining olive oil to make the salsa slightly sloppy. Season to taste with black pepper.

fresh tomato salsa

500 g ripe tomatoes, skinned and finely diced

½ red onion, finely chopped

1–2 small green chillies, deseeded and finely chopped

3 tablespoons freshly squeezed lime juice

a pinch of caster sugar

2 tablespoons finely chopped fresh coriander

sea salt

SERVES 4

Put the tomatoes in a large bowl with the onion and chillies. Add the lime juice and mix well, then add the sugar and season with salt. When ready to serve, add the coriander.

barbecue sauce

200 ml tomato passata
100 ml maple syrup
50 ml dark treacle
50 ml tomato ketchup
50 ml white wine vinegar
3 tablespoons Worcestershire sauce
1 tablespoon Dijon mustard
1 teaspoon garlic powder
¼ teaspoon hot paprika
sea salt and freshly ground black pepper

MAKES ABOUT 400 ML

Put all the ingredients into a small saucepan, bring to the boil and simmer gently for 10–15 minutes until reduced slightly and thickened. Season to taste with salt and pepper and let cool.

Pour into an airtight container and store in the refrigerator for up to 2 weeks.

sweet chilli sauce

6 large red chillies, deseeded and chopped
4 garlic cloves, chopped
1 teaspoon grated fresh ginger
1 teaspoon sea salt
100 ml rice wine vinegar
100 ml sugar

MAKES ABOUT 200 ML

Put the chillies, garlic, ginger and salt into a food processor and blend to a coarse paste. Transfer to a saucepan, add the vinegar and sugar, bring to the boil and simmer gently, part-covered, for 5 minutes until the mixture becomes a thin syrup. Remove from the heat and let cool.

Pour into an airtight container and store in the refrigerator for up to 2 weeks.

Asian barbecue sauce

100 ml tomato passata
50 ml hoisin sauce
1 teaspoon hot chilli sauce
2 garlic cloves, crushed
2 tablespoons sweet soy sauce
1 tablespoon rice wine vinegar
1 teaspoon ground coriander
½ teaspoon ground cinnamon
¼ teaspoon Chinese five-spice powder

MAKES ABOUT 350 ML

Put all the ingredients into a small saucepan, add 100 ml water, bring to the boil and simmer gently for 10 minutes. Remove from the heat and let cool.

Pour into an airtight container and store in the refrigerator for up to 2 weeks.

creamy corn salsa

1 corn cob, husk removed

2 red chillies

1 tomato, diced

1 garlic clove, crushed

freshly squeezed juice of ½ lime

1 tablespoon maple syrup

2 tablespoons soured cream

sea salt and freshly ground
black pepper

SERVES 6

Preheat the barbecue or grill until hot. Add the corn and cook for about 15 minutes, turning frequently, until charred on all sides. Let cool.

Add the chillies and grill until the skins are charred all over. Transfer to a bowl and cover with a clean cloth until cool.

Using a sharp knife, cut down all sides of the corn cob to remove the kernels. Put them into a bowl. Peel and deseed the chillies, chop the flesh and add it to the corn.

Stir in all the remaining ingredients, season to taste, then serve.

hot pineapple and papaya salsa

½ ripe pineapple

½ large papaya

1–2 green chillies, deseeded
and chopped

2 spring onions, finely chopped

1 tablespoon chopped fresh mint

freshly squeezed juice of 1 lime

1 tablespoon Thai fish sauce

SERVES 6

Peel the pineapple, remove and discard the core, then dice the flesh and put into a serving bowl, together with any juice.

Peel the papaya, scoop out the seeds and dice the flesh. Add to the pineapple.

Stir in the chillies, spring onions, mint, lime juice and fish sauce, and set aside to infuse for about 30 minutes, then serve.

tomato, sesame and ginger salsa

2 ripe tomatoes, peeled, deseeded
and diced

½ red onion, finely chopped

5 cm fresh ginger, peeled and grated

1 garlic clove, chopped

1 tablespoon chopped fresh
coriander

2 tablespoons peanut oil

1 tablespoon soy sauce

1 teaspoon sesame oil

SERVES 6

Put all the ingredients into a bowl, set aside to infuse for about 30 minutes, then serve.

grilled pepper butter sauce

Grilling the pepper until the skin chars and blackens makes it easier to peel and also gives the sauce a gorgeous smoky flavour.

1 large red pepper

75 g unsalted butter, diced

1 tablespoon freshly squeezed lime juice

a pinch of saffron threads

a pinch of cayenne pepper

sea salt and freshly ground black pepper

SERVES 4

Grill the red pepper for 8–10 minutes, or until tender and charred all over. Seal in a plastic bag and leave until cool enough to handle.

Skin and deseed the pepper, chop the flesh and put in a saucepan with the butter, lime juice, saffron and cayenne. Heat through until the butter has melted.

Using a food processor or hand blender, process the pepper mixture until smooth. Season to taste. Serve hot.

piri-piri sauce

Piri-piri is a condiment used in Portuguese cooking. It was introduced into Africa by the Portuguese, hence its Swahili name which translates as 'chilli' (or 'chilli-chilli'). It is lovely drizzled over barbecued chicken, or wonderful with char-grilled squid or prawns.

8 red bird's-eye chillies

300 ml extra virgin olive oil

1 tablespoon white wine vinegar

a pinch of sea salt

MAKES ABOUT 300 ML

Finely chop the chillies (including the seeds) and put in a bowl. Add the olive oil, vinegar and salt.

Transfer to a sterilized bottle (see page 39) and store in a cool place for up to 1 week.

smoky barbecue sauce

A good barbecue sauce should be tangy, smoky and rich, just like this one. Serve in burgers or with barbecued beef, lamb or chicken.

200 ml passata

100 ml maple syrup

50 ml black treacle

50 ml tomato ketchup

50 ml malt vinegar

3 tablespoons Worcestershire sauce

1 tablespoon Dijon mustard

1 teaspoon garlic powder

a pinch of smoked paprika

sea salt and freshly ground black pepper

MAKES ABOUT 400 ML

Put all the ingredients in a small saucepan, bring to the boil and simmer gently for 10–15 minutes, or until reduced slightly, and thickened. Season to taste.

Pour into a sterilized bottle (see page 39) and refrigerate for up to 2 weeks.

Flavouring butter with herbs, spices and aromatics provides a great staple to have on hand at a barbecue. You can add an almost endless amount of flavourings to butter to serve with any type of meat, fish or vegetables. Try the suggestions below or experiment with flavours of your own choice.

caper butter

2 tablespoons capers in brine, drained and dried

125 g unsalted butter, softened

1 tablespoon chopped fresh flat leaf parsley

1 teaspoon finely grated lemon zest

freshly ground black pepper

SERVES 4–6

Finely chop the capers and put in a bowl with the butter, parsley, lemon zest and pepper. Beat together with a fork until evenly combined.

Transfer the butter to a small piece of greaseproof paper and roll into a log. Wrap the paper around the butter and twist the ends to seal. Refrigerate or freeze until required. Serve in slices.

saffron butter

a large pinch of saffron threads

125 g unsalted butter, softened

sea salt and freshly ground black pepper

SERVES 4–6

Soak the saffron in 1 teaspoon of boiling water for 10 minutes, then beat into the butter and season. Transfer to a small piece of greaseproof paper and continue to follow the recipe for caper butter.

herb butter

2 tablespoons chopped fresh herbs such as basil, chives, dill, mint or parsley

125 g unsalted butter, softened

sea salt and freshly ground black pepper

SERVES 4–6

Beat the herbs and seasoning into the butter until evenly combined. Transfer to a small piece of greaseproof paper and continue to follow the recipe for caper butter.

baba ganoush

3 aubergines

4 tablespoons plain yoghurt

2 tablespoons tahini paste

1 garlic clove, crushed

1 teaspoon salt

freshly squeezed juice of 1–2 lemons, to taste

1 tablespoon finely chopped fresh flat leaf parsley (optional)

pita breads, warmed or lightly toasted on the barbecue, to serve

SERVES 8

Baba ganoush is the famous creamy aubergine purée with smoky overtones. It's best to char them over the barbecue to achieve the authentic smoky flavour, but, if you want to prepare it in advance, a hot grill or the open flame on a gas hob are also fine. Serve baba ganoush as a dip or with other dishes as a first course.

Put the aubergines on the barbecue grill or over the open gas flame on top of the stove and cook until well charred on all sides. The steam created inside the vegetable will cook the flesh. The aubergines must be charred all over and soft in the middle. Remove from the flame and let cool on a plate.

When cool, carefully pull off the skins and stems. Don't leave any charred bits. Put the flesh into a bowl, then blend with a hand-held stick blender or potato masher: the texture should not be too smooth. Add the yoghurt, tahini, garlic and salt and blend again.

Add the juice of 1 lemon, taste, then gradually add more juice until you achieve flavour and texture to your taste. Transfer to a serving bowl and sprinkle with finely chopped parsley, if using.

Serve with wedges of toasted pita breads for scooping the dip.

tzatziki

½ cucumber, deseeded
and grated

2 teaspoons sea salt

1 garlic clove, crushed (optional)

150 ml Greek yoghurt

freshly squeezed juice of ½ lemon

MAKES ABOUT 250 ML

Greek tzatziki is a versatile dip that also makes a great salad dressing or accompaniment to barbecued chicken and fish or vegetables.

Mix the grated cucumber and salt together and let stand for 10 minutes. Put the cucumber in the centre of a clean tea towel, gather up the edges and twist to squeeze as much moisture out as possible. Put the cucumber in a bowl with the remaining ingredients and stir to combine. The tzatziki will keep in the refrigerator for 3 days.

Variations

Beetroot tzatziki Add 1 medium raw or 2 bottled beetroot, grated, and 2 tablespoons chopped chives to the mixture. This makes a great accompaniment to boiled new potatoes.

Spiced tzatziki Put 2 teaspoons cumin seeds and 2 teaspoons coriander seeds in a hot, dry frying pan and heat, stirring continuously, for about 30 seconds until fragrant. Transfer to a mortar and pestle and grind to a powder. Add to the tzatziki along with 1 teaspoon paprika.

Olive tzatziki Stir 75–100 g finely chopped stoned black or green olives into the yoghurt and cucumber mixture.

guacamole

3 medium, ripe avocados, halved, stoned and peeled

2 tablespoons freshly squeezed lime juice

1 small red onion, very finely chopped

1–2 green chillies, very finely chopped

1 tomato, deseeded and finely chopped

sea salt

tortilla chips or bread sticks, to serve

MAKES ABOUT 500 ML

This popular Mexican dip can be made in many ways. This recipe contains all the popular ingredients, but feel free to leave out any you don't like. Adjust the chillies according to your taste.

Put the avocado flesh in a bowl with the lime juice and crush to a rough purée with a fork (if you like a smooth purée, you can blend the avocado and lime juice together in a food processor, then transfer to a bowl).

Add the onion, chillies and tomato and mix until combined. Season to taste with salt. The guacamole will discolour quickly, so is best eaten on the day of making.

Variations

Herbed guacamole Add 2 teaspoons each of finely chopped coriander, mint and parsley to the guacamole for a pungent, refreshing dip.

Feta and avocado dip Add 75 g finely crumbled feta cheese to the guacamole. This is great served with pita crisps.

parsley, feta and pine nut dip

Flat leaf parsley leaves have such a delightful flavour, they make this dip beautifully fragrant. Serve with a selection of crisp raw vegetables or as an accompaniment to grilled fish.

50 g fresh flat leaf parsley leaves

1 garlic clove, peeled and crushed

75 g pine nuts, toasted

100 g feta cheese, diced

150 ml extra virgin olive oil

freshly ground black pepper

SERVES 6–8

Put all the ingredients in a food processor and blend to form a fairly smooth sauce. Season to taste, cover and set aside to infuse for 30 minutes before serving. Store in a screw-top jar in the refrigerator for up to 3 days.

chilli tomato chutney

This versatile, tangy chutney is great with grilled meat or poultry.

1 small piece of dried chilli, to taste

4 cm fresh ginger, peeled and coarsely chopped

2 garlic cloves

2 shallots

125 ml white wine vinegar

1 kg canned whole plum tomatoes, drained, juice reserved, deseeded and chopped

200 g demerara sugar

MAKES 500 G

Put the chilli, ginger, garlic and shallots in a food processor and chop finely. Put the vinegar, tomatoes and sugar into a large, heavy saucepan, add the ginger mixture and stir well.

Put the saucepan over medium heat, bring slowly to the boil, then simmer over low heat for 1½ hours or until reduced by half, stirring from time to time. Should the chutney dry out too much, add a little of the reserved tomato juice. Let cool a little, then spoon into a sterilized jam jar and seal with a screw-top lid.

Pictured on page 37, top right

peperonata

2 onions, thinly sliced

a large handful of fresh parsley, finely chopped, plus extra to serve

2 red peppers, deseeded and sliced

2 yellow peppers, deseeded and sliced

1 kg canned whole plum tomatoes, drained, deseeded and chopped

sea salt and freshly ground black pepper

olive oil, for frying

SERVES 8

Cover the base of a heavy-based frying pan with olive oil and put over medium heat. Add the onion and parsley and fry until the onion is softened, but not browned. Add the peppers, cook until soft, then add the tomatoes. Reduce the heat, cover and cook for 1 hour, stirring from time to time. Season with salt and pepper to taste.

Serve hot or cold, sprinkled with parsley, with barbecued fish, seafood, poultry or meat.

mango, kiwi and coriander salsa

1 large ripe mango, peeled, stoned and cut into 1–2 cm cubes

4 kiwi fruit, peeled and cut into 1 cm cubes

finely grated zest and freshly squeezed juice of ½ unwaxed lemon

1 tablespoon extra virgin olive oil

1 tablespoon finely chopped fresh coriander

sea salt and freshly ground black pepper

SERVES 4

Put the mango and kiwi fruit in a glass bowl, then add the lemon zest and juice, olive oil and coriander. Season with salt and pepper to taste and mix well. Cover and refrigerate until required. Serve with barbecued seafood, chicken or lamb.

parsley and anchovy relish

6 anchovy fillets

1 tablespoon salted capers, rinsed well and dried

a large handful of fresh parsley

grated zest of 1 unwaxed lemon

2 garlic cloves

4 tablespoons extra virgin olive oil

SERVES 4

Put the anchovies, capers, parsley, lemon zest and garlic on a chopping board and chop together with a large kitchen knife so that all the ingredients remain identifiable but tiny. Alternatively, put the ingredients in a food processor and chop finely, but take care not to reduce them to a mush.

Transfer to a bowl and stir in the olive oil. Cover and refrigerate until required. Serve with barbecued meat or fish.

tomato, lemon and courgette relish

2 small unwaxed lemons

500 g courgettes, finely chopped

2 red or white onions, finely chopped

4 tablespoons sea salt

1 kg tomatoes, chopped

150 g sugar

375 ml white wine vinegar or cider vinegar

1 tablespoon white mustard seeds

1 teaspoon dill seeds or celery seeds

¼ teaspoon turmeric

MAKES ABOUT 1.25 LITRES

Pickled or preserved lemons develop such a unique and wonderful flavour that is captured in this tomato and courgette relish. It makes a great accompaniment to sausages, lamb and chicken, but it really goes with practically anything!

Carefully cut the rind from the lemons, with a very thin layer of white pith. Finely chop and put in a glass or ceramic bowl with the juice from 1 of the lemons. Put the courgettes and onions in separate bowls. Sprinkle each with the salt, cover and leave at room temperature overnight. When ready to make the relish, rinse well with cold water and drain thoroughly.

Put the tomatoes, sugar and vinegar in a large saucepan and bring to the boil, stirring constantly to dissolve the sugar. Reduce to a simmer and cook for 1 hour, stirring occasionally, until thick. Bring back to the boil and add the drained lemon rind, courgettes and onions with the mustard seeds, dill seeds and turmeric. Cook for 5 minutes. Spoon into sterilized jars and seal. The relish will keep for up to 1 year if sealed correctly.

Note Always sterilize preserving jars before use. Wash them in hot, soapy water and rinse in boiling water. Place in a large saucepan and then cover with hot water. With the lid on, bring the water to the boil and continue boiling for 15 minutes. Turn off the heat, then leave the jars in the hot water until just before they are to be filled. Invert the jars onto clean kitchen paper to dry. Sterilize the lids for 5 minutes, by boiling, or according to the manufacturers' instructions. Jars should be filled and sealed while they are still hot.

sweet chilli and tomato salsa

2 tablespoons sesame seeds

1 teaspoon Szechuan peppercorns

a small bunch of fresh coriander, stems and leaves

3 garlic cloves, peeled

2 large, mild red chillies, stems removed

3 cm fresh ginger, peeled

100 g caster sugar

2 tablespoons freshly squeezed lime juice

1 tablespoon soy sauce

4 tomatoes, chopped

MAKES ABOUT 400 ML

This is an Asian-inspired salsa with a sweet and spicy flavour. It can be served as a dip with rice or prawn crackers or vegetable crisps, or as an accompaniment to grilled shellfish, fish, chicken, pork or duck.

Heat a frying pan to medium, add the sesame seeds and toast, tossing the pan, until golden. Set aside.

In the same frying pan, toast the Szechuan peppercorns for 3 minutes, stirring, until just fragrant. Let cool, transfer to a mortar and pestle and roughly grind. Put the Szechuan pepper in a mini food processor with the coriander stems, garlic, chillies and ginger and process to a paste.

Put the sugar in a saucepan with a little water and bring to the boil, stirring until dissolved. Boil undisturbed for 1 minute, stir in the chilli and ginger paste and remove from the heat. Let cool.

In a bowl, mix together the sugar syrup and chilli paste mixture, lime juice, soy sauce, chopped tomatoes, coriander leaves and sesame seeds. The salsa will keep in the refrigerator for 3 days.

chilli jam

This fiery jam is a really useful ingredient to have in your storecupboard and it is so much better than the shop-bought varieties. It is hot, but the sweetness tempers this beautifully. It will store for a long time. Serve with Thai fishcakes or barbecued prawns.

500 g ripe tomatoes, roughly chopped

4 red bird's-eye chillies, roughly chopped

2 garlic cloves, peeled

1 teaspoon grated fresh ginger

2 tablespoons light soy sauce

200 g grated palm sugar

75 ml white wine vinegar

½ teaspoon sea salt

MAKES ABOUT 300 ML

Put the tomatoes, chillies and garlic in a food processor and process until quite smooth. Transfer to a saucepan and add the remaining ingredients. Bring to the boil and simmer gently, stirring occasionally, for 30–40 minutes, or until thick and jam-like.

Spoon into a sterilized bottle or jar (see page 39) and leave to cool, then seal. Refrigerate once opened.

roast garlic, paprika and sherry alioli

Spanish-style alioli is great as a dipping sauce for seafood and vegetables or a good accompaniment to barbecued vegetables and meats.

1 whole garlic bulb

2 egg yolks

1 tablespoon sherry vinegar

¼ teaspoon sea salt

¼ teaspoon smoked paprika

190 ml light-flavoured oil, such as grapeseed or vegetable

1 tablespoon sherry

MAKES ABOUT 200 ML

Preheat the oven to 180°C (350°F) Gas 4.

Cut 1 cm off the top of the garlic bulb and discard. Loosely wrap the garlic in foil and roast in the preheated oven for 45 minutes until very soft. Let cool, then press the softened cloves from the skins. Crush the cloves on a chopping board with the side of a large knife to form a paste.

In a bowl, whisk together the garlic with the egg yolks, vinegar, salt and paprika. Add the oil, drop by drop, whisking continuously until emulsified and thick. Finally whisk in the sherry. The alioli will keep in the refrigerator for 2–3 days.

2 kg tomatoes

3 teaspoons sea salt

leaves from a small bunch
of fresh thyme

2 tablespoons olive oil

1 white onion, chopped

1 teaspoon whole allspice berries

½ teaspoon whole cloves

½ teaspoon black peppercorns

400 g sugar

1 teaspoon dry mustard powder

500 ml cider vinegar

MAKES ABOUT 1.5 LITRES

roast tomato ketchup

**Homemade tomato ketchup captures the true flavour
of ripe tomatoes in season. Slow-roasting the tomatoes
results in a more intense flavour, but one that is not as
full-on as barbecue sauce.**

Preheat the oven to 150°C (300°F) Gas 2.

Cut the tomatoes in half and arrange cut-side up in a roasting tin.
Sprinkle with 2 teaspoons of the salt and all the thyme leaves and
drizzle with 1 tablespoon of the oil. Roast in the preheated oven
for 1½ hours.

Heat the remaining oil in a large saucepan over medium heat,
add the onion and sauté for 10 minutes until golden.

Put the allspice, cloves and peppercorns in a mortar and pestle
and grind to a powder. Add to the onion and cook for 1 minute.
Add the roasted tomatoes, sugar, mustard powder, vinegar and
remaining teaspoon salt and bring to the boil. Adjust the heat to
a steady low boil and cook for 30 minutes, uncovered, stirring
occasionally to prevent burning.

Blend to a thick sauce using a stick blender or transfer to a
blender. Transfer into sterilized bottles and seal (see note on
page 39). The ketchup will keep for up to 1 year if properly
sealed and stored in a cool, dark place.

meat dishes

cheeseburger

750 g chuck steak, minced

1 onion, finely chopped

1 garlic clove, crushed

2 teaspoons chopped fresh thyme

125 g Cheddar cheese, sliced

4 burger buns, halved

4 tablespoons Mayonnaise
(see page 199)

4 large leaves of butter lettuce

2 tomatoes, sliced

½ red onion, thinly sliced

sea salt and freshly ground
black pepper

olive oil, for brushing

SERVES 4

This version of a cheeseburger avoids the usual processed cheese slices in favour of a good-quality cheese – and tastes all the better for it. You can vary the cheese to your own taste – whether a traditional Cheddar or, if you are feeling adventurous, a Camembert or crumbled Roquefort.

Put the beef, onion, garlic, thyme and some salt and pepper in a bowl and work together with your hands until evenly mixed and slightly sticky. Divide into 4 portions and shape into patties. Cover and chill for 30 minutes.

Preheat the barbecue. Brush the patties lightly with olive oil and barbecue for 5 minutes on each side until lightly charred and cooked through. Top the patties with the cheese slices and set under a hot grill for 30 seconds until the cheese has melted. Keep them warm.

Toast the buns, then spread each base and top with mayonnaise. Add the lettuce leaves, cheese-topped patties and tomato and onion slices. Add the bun tops and serve hot.

Kids love burgers and these are served as sausage shapes in a hot dog roll. Alternatively, shape as the more traditional patties and serve in small toasted buns. You can add some shredded lettuce and tomatoes to the burger for a healthier option.

'sausage' burgers for kids

500 g premium beef mince

2 teaspoons onion powder

2 tablespoons Roast Tomato Ketchup (page 44 or you can use shop-bought ketchup), plus extra to serve

2 tablespoons chopped fresh flat leaf parsley

8 hot dog rolls

100 g grated Cheddar cheese

sea salt and freshly ground black pepper

olive oil, for brushing

SERVES 4

Put the beef, onion powder, tomato ketchup, parsley and a little salt and pepper in a bowl and work together with your hands until evenly mixed. Divide into 4 portions and form long thin sausage shapes. Cover and chill for 30 minutes.

Preheat the barbecue. Brush the 'sausage' burgers lightly with olive oil and barbecue for 7–8 minutes, turning frequently until cooked through.

Split the rolls horizontally without cutting all the way through. Put a 'sausage' into each one and sprinkle with some grated cheese and tomato ketchup. Serve hot.*

open Tex-Mex burger
with chilli relish

750 g beef chuck steak, minced

1 small red onion, finely chopped

1 garlic clove, crushed

2 teaspoons dried oregano

1½ teaspoons ground cumin

2 burger buns, halved

100 g shredded iceberg lettuce

100 g grated Cheddar cheese

sea salt and freshly ground
black pepper

olive oil, for brushing

Chilli relish

500 g tomatoes,
coarsely chopped

1 red onion, coarsely chopped

2 garlic cloves, crushed

2–4 jalapeño chillies,
coarsely chopped

2 tablespoons
Worcestershire sauce

200 g soft brown sugar

150 ml red wine vinegar

2 teaspoons sea salt

SERVES 4

**The flavours of Texas and Mexico combine well in this
tangy burger and for those who really like it hot, try the
Caribbean version with the fiery chilli sauce.**

To make the chilli relish, put the tomatoes, onion, garlic and
chillies in a food processor and blend until smooth. Transfer the
mixture to a saucepan, add the Worcestershire sauce, sugar,
vinegar and the 2 teaspoons of salt. Bring to the boil and simmer
gently for 30–40 minutes until the sauce has thickened. Let cool
completely and refrigerate until required.

Put the beef, onion, garlic, oregano, cumin and some salt and
pepper in a bowl and work together with your hands until slightly
sticky and evenly mixed. Divide into 4 portions and shape into
patties. Cover and chill for 30 minutes.

Preheat the barbecue. Brush the patties lightly with olive oil
and barbecue or grill for 4–5 minutes on each side until cooked
through. Keep them warm.

Lightly toast the buns. Top each half with shredded lettuce, a
patty, some grated cheese and chilli relish. Serve hot.

Variation
Caribbean Chilli Burger Make the chilli relish as above, replacing
the jalapeño chillies with 1 Scotch bonnet or habanero chilli,
seeded and chopped. When assembling the burger, add a layer
of sliced avocado to help to temper the fire of the extra-hot chilli
sauce (use disposable latex gloves when handling Scotch bonnet
or habanero chillies).

Beef satay

500 g beef sirloin,
sliced against the grain into
bite-sized pieces

1 tablespoon peanut oil

Peanut sauce

60 ml peanut or
vegetable oil

4–5 garlic cloves, crushed

4–5 dried serrano chillies,
deseeded and ground using
a pestle and mortar

1–2 teaspoons curry powder

60 g roasted peanuts,
finely ground

To serve

a small bunch of fresh coriander

a small bunch of fresh mint

lime wedges

*a packet of short wooden or
bamboo skewers, soaked in
water before use*

SERVES 4–6

fiery beef satay
in peanut sauce

**Beef, pork or chicken satays cooked in, or served
with, a fiery peanut sauce are hugely popular throughout
Southeast Asia. This particular sauce is a great favourite
in Thailand, Vietnam and Indonesia. It is best to make
your own but commercial brands are available under
the banner satay or sate sauce.**

To make the sauce, heat the oil in a heavy-based saucepan and
stir in the garlic until it begins to colour. Add the chillies, curry
powder and the peanuts and stir over a gentle heat, until the
mixture forms a paste. Remove from the heat and leave to cool.

Put the beef pieces in a bowl. Beat the peanut oil into the sauce
and tip the mixture onto the beef. Mix well, so that the beef is
evenly coated and thread the meat onto the prepared skewers.

Preheat the barbecue. Cook the satays for 2–3 minutes on each
side, then serve the skewered meat with the lime wedges and
fresh herbs to wrap around each tasty morsel.

spicy beef and coconut kofta kebabs

1 teaspoon coriander seeds

1 teaspoon cumin seeds

175 g desiccated or freshly grated coconut, plus 2–3 tablespoons, to serve

1 tablespoon coconut oil

4 shallots, peeled and finely chopped

2 garlic cloves, finely chopped

1–2 fresh red chillies, deseeded and finely chopped

350 g lean minced beef

1 beaten egg, to bind

sea salt and freshly ground black pepper

lime wedges, to serve

a packet of short wooden or bamboo skewers, soaked in water before use

SERVES 4

Variations of this Asian dish can be found at street stalls from Sri Lanka to the Philippines and South Africa to the West Indies. Simple and tasty, the kofta are delicious barbecued and served with wedges of fresh lime or a dipping sauce of your choice.

In a small heavy-based frying pan, dry roast the coriander and cumin seeds until they give off a nutty aroma. Using a mortar and pestle, or a spice grinder, grind the roasted seeds to a powder.

In the same pan, dry roast the coconut until it begins to colour and give off a nutty aroma. Tip it onto a plate to cool, reserving 2–3 tablespoons.

Heat the coconut oil in the same small heavy-based pan and stir in the shallots, garlic and chillies, until fragrant and beginning to colour. Tip them onto a plate to cool.

Put the minced beef in a bowl and add the ground spices, toasted coconut and shallot mixture. Season with salt and pepper and use a fork to mix all the ingredients together, adding a little egg to bind it (you may not need it all). Knead the mixture with your hands and mould it into little balls. Thread the balls onto the prepared skewers.

Preheat the barbecue. Cook the kebabs for 3–4 minutes on each side. Sprinkle the cooked kofta with the reserved toasted coconut and serve with the wedges of lime to squeeze over them.

Tuscan-style steak

1 large T-bone steak, about 700 g
and cut to an even thickness
of 2.5–3 cm

100 ml olive oil

2 garlic cloves, thinly sliced

3 sprigs of fresh rosemary

sea salt and freshly ground
black pepper

good-quality extra virgin olive oil,
for drizzling

To serve

sautéed potatoes

rocket salad

lemon wedges (optional)

SERVES 2

The traditional cut to use for this classic Tuscan recipe, known locally as Bistecca alla Fiorentina, is a T-bone steak, marinated overnight in olive oil and garlic and cooked over a charcoal barbecue. You could also use a gas barbecue – either way, it's a treat for any meat lover!

Trim the excess fat off the edge of the steak, leaving a little if liked, and pat the steak dry with kitchen paper. Pour the measured olive oil into a shallow dish and add the garlic and rosemary. Turn the steak in the oil, ensuring there is some garlic and rosemary on each side. Cover with a double layer of clingfilm and let marinate in the refrigerator for 24 hours, turning a couple of times. Bring to room temperature before cooking it.

Preheat the barbecue. Take the meat out of the marinade and remove any pieces of garlic or rosemary from the steak. Pat dry with kitchen paper. Put the steak on a rack about 8 cm above the coals and cook for about 4 minutes. Turn the steak over and cook for a further 3 minutes. (Cook for a couple of minutes longer on each side for a medium-rare steak, although this is traditionally served rare.)

Transfer to a warm plate and season both sides with salt and pepper. Cover lightly with aluminium foil, then let rest for 5 minutes.

Stand the steak upright with the bone at the bottom and, using a sharp knife, remove the meat either side of the bone in one piece. Cut the meat into slices, 0.5–1 cm thick. Divide the slices between 2 serving plates. Pour over any meat juices that have accumulated under the meat and drizzle with the best extra virgin olive oil you can lay your hands on.

Serve with sautéed potatoes, a rocket salad and lemon wedges.

Argentinian-style 'asado' steak
with chimichurri salsa

a whole piece of sirloin,
1.5–1.75 kg

olive oil, for rubbing and brushing

sea salt

roasted new potatoes*, to serve

green salad, to serve

Chimichurri salsa

150 ml olive oil

75 ml red wine vinegar

1 teaspoon dried oregano

4–5 tablespoons chopped fresh
flat leaf parsley, stalks removed
and chopped

½–1 teaspoon crushed
dried chillies

2 large garlic cloves,
finely chopped

1 bay leaf

150 ml salmuera (salt water
solution made from 1 rounded
tablespoon sea salt dissolved in
150 ml warm water and cooled)

SERVES 8–10

Serve juicy steak Argentinian style with the classic accompaniment of chimichurri salsa – a punchy, garlic dressing that needs to be made the day before for the flavours to fully develop.

To make the chimichurri salsa, put the olive oil, vinegar, oregano, parsley, crushed dried chillies, garlic, bay leaf and salmuera in a screw-top jar and shake well. Chill overnight in the refrigerator. Bring to room temperature before serving.

Trim the meat of excess fat, then rub lightly with olive oil and sprinkle with salt. Preheat a charcoal barbecue and let it burn until the flames have completely died down and the ash is a powdery white. Put the beef on a rack 8 cm above the hot coals. Cook for 15–20 minutes for a rare steak or 25–30 minutes for a medium-rare steak, turning every 4–5 minutes. If the meat seems to be drying out, brush over a little extra oil. Transfer to a warm plate, cover lightly with aluminium foil and let rest for 5–10 minutes.

Cut the steak into thick slices and serve a couple of slices on each plate. Shake the chimichurri salsa vigorously and splash over the steaks. Serve with roasted new potatoes and a green salad.

*Note To make roasted new potatoes, put 1 kg halved new potatoes in a roasting tin with 75 ml olive oil, 4 sprigs of fresh rosemary and 6–8 garlic cloves. Roast in a preheated oven at 180°C (350°F) Gas 4 for about 45 minutes, turning occasionally.

Steak and blue cheese complement each other perfectly as the cheese brings out the taste of the beef. This dish is made even more special when combined with the smoky char-grilled flavours of the barbecue.

4 fillet steaks, 200 g each

sea salt and freshly ground black pepper

baby spinach salad, to serve

Blue cheese butter

50 g unsalted butter, softened

50 g soft blue cheese, such as Gorgonzola

25 g walnuts, finely ground in a blender

2 tablespoons chopped fresh parsley

sea salt and freshly ground black pepper

SERVES 4

steak with blue cheese butter

To make the blue cheese butter, put the butter, cheese, walnuts and parsley into a bowl and beat well. Season to taste. Form into a log, wrap in a piece of greaseproof paper, twist the ends to seal and chill for about 30 minutes.

Lightly season the steaks and cook on a preheated barbecue (or pan-fry in a little oil) for 3 minutes on each side for rare, or 4–5 minutes for medium to well done.

Cut the butter into 8 slices. Put 2 slices of butter onto each cooked steak, wrap loosely with foil and let rest for 5 minutes.

Serve the steaks with a salad of baby spinach.

2 long, thin pieces of bavette (skirt steak), about 175–200 g each, or 350–400 g minute steak

8 flour tortillas

crisp cos lettuce leaves, shredded

Marinade

3 tablespoons freshly squeezed lime juice

1 garlic clove, crushed

1 teaspoon mild chilli powder

3 tablespoons light olive oil or sunflower oil

Chunky guacamole

2 large avocados, about 200 g each

2 tablespoons freshly squeezed lime juice

4 spring onions, trimmed and thinly sliced

1 garlic clove, crushed

1 small green chilli, deseeded and thinly sliced (optional)

1 tablespoon olive oil

2–3 tomatoes, about 175 g, skinned, deseeded and chopped

3 tablespoons chopped coriander leaves

sea salt

SERVES 4

char-grilled steak fajitas
with chunky guacamole

The word fajitas, meaning straps, actually refers to the cut of beef that is traditionally used for this classic Tex-Mex dish, which is cooked over an open fire. If you want to use the authentic cut, a skirt steak, you'll probably need to order it from a butcher in advance.

To make the marinade, put the lime juice, garlic and chilli powder in a shallow dish and whisk together. Gradually whisk in the olive oil. Put the steaks in the marinade and turn so that they are thoroughly coated. Cover and let marinate for 30 minutes while you prepare and light the barbecue.

Meanwhile, to make the guacamole, scoop out the flesh from the avocados and put it in a bowl with the lime juice. Chop with a knife to give a chunky consistency. Add the spring onions, garlic, chilli, if using, and olive oil and mix well. Add the tomatoes, coriander and salt, cover and set aside.

When the barbecue flames have completely died down and ash is white, pat the steak dry with kitchen paper and cook for about 1½ minutes each side. Set aside and let rest for 3–4 minutes while you warm the tortillas in a dry frying pan. Thinly slice the steak, then put a dollop of guacamole on each tortilla and top with slices of steak and shredded lettuce leaves. Carefully roll up the tortillas, press together and cut in half diagonally.

650 g boneless lamb shoulder, cut into 2 cm cubes

100 g pork belly, chopped

1 onion, very finely chopped

2 garlic cloves, crushed

2 tablespoons ground cumin

2 teaspoons ground cinnamon

1 tablespoon dried oregano

2 teaspoons sea salt

50 g fresh breadcrumbs

1 tablespoon capers, drained and chopped

1 large egg, beaten

freshly ground black pepper

Mint yoghurt

200 g thick natural yoghurt

2 tablespoons chopped fresh mint

sea salt and freshly ground black pepper

To serve

4 crusty rolls

salad leaves

tomato slices

SERVES 4

lamb burgers
with mint yoghurt

A good burger should be thick, moist, tender and juicy. These lamb burgers are all that and more. Serve in crusty rolls with a few slices of tomato, plenty of fresh salad leaves and a generous spoonful of the cool minty yoghurt dressing. The perfect burger for a barbecue party.

Put the lamb and pork into a food processor and process briefly until coarsely ground. Transfer to a bowl and, using your hands, work in the chopped onion, garlic, cumin, cinnamon, oregano, salt, breadcrumbs, capers, beaten egg and pepper. Cover and let marinate in the refrigerator for at least 2 hours.

Put the yoghurt into a bowl and stir in the mint, then add a little salt and pepper to taste. Set aside until required.

Using damp hands, shape the meat into 8 burgers. Preheat the barbecue, then brush the grill rack with oil. Cook the burgers for about 3 minutes on each side.

Split the rolls in half and fill with the cooked burgers, salad leaves, tomato slices and a spoonful of mint yoghurt.

Variation

For a traditional hamburger, replace the lamb with beef, omit the spices and, instead of the capers, add 4 chopped anchovy fillets. Serve in burger buns with salad.

butterflied lamb
with white bean salad

This is probably the best way to cook lamb on the barbecue – the bone is removed and the meat opened out flat so it can cook quickly and evenly over the coals. If you don't fancy boning the lamb yourself, ask the butcher to do it for you.

1.5–2 kg leg of lamb, butterflied

1 recipe Herb, Lemon and Garlic Marinade (page 15)

1 recipe Salsa Verde (page 19), to serve

White bean salad

1 large red onion, finely chopped

3 cans haricot beans, about 400 g each, drained

2 garlic cloves, chopped

3 tomatoes, deseeded and chopped

75 ml extra virgin olive oil

1½ tablespoons red wine vinegar

2 tablespoons chopped fresh parsley

sea salt and freshly ground black pepper

SERVES 8

To make the salad, put the onion into a colander, sprinkle with salt and let drain over a bowl for 30 minutes. Wash the onion under cold running water and dry well. Transfer to a bowl, then add the beans, garlic, tomatoes, olive oil, vinegar, parsley and salt and pepper to taste.

Put the lamb into a shallow dish, pour over the marinade, cover and let marinate in the refrigerator overnight. Remove from the refrigerator 1 hour before cooking.

Preheat the barbecue. Drain the lamb and discard the marinade. Cook over medium hot coals for 12–15 minutes on each side until charred on the outside but still pink in the middle (cook for a little longer if you prefer the meat less rare). Let the lamb rest for 10 minutes.

Cut the lamb into slices and serve with the white bean salad and salsa verde.

1 kg neck end of lamb

1 tablespoon chopped
fresh rosemary

1 tablespoon dried oregano

1 onion, chopped

4 garlic cloves, chopped

300 ml red wine

freshly squeezed juice of 1 lemon

75 ml olive oil

sea salt and freshly ground
black pepper

Cracked wheat salad

350 g cracked wheat
(bulghur wheat)

25 g fresh parsley

15 g fresh mint leaves

2 garlic cloves, crushed

150 ml extra virgin olive oil

freshly squeezed juice of 2 lemons

a pinch of caster sugar

sea salt and freshly ground
black pepper

*6 large rosemary stalks or
metal skewers*

SERVES 6

souvlaki with
cracked wheat salad

Souvlaki is the classic Greek kebab, a delicious combination of cubed lamb marinated in red wine with herbs and lemon juice. The meat is tenderized by the wine, resulting in a juicy and succulent dish.

Trim any large pieces of fat from the lamb and then cut the meat into 2.5 cm cubes. Put into a shallow, non-metal dish. Add the rosemary, oregano, onion, garlic, wine, lemon juice, olive oil, salt and pepper. Toss well, cover and leave to marinate in the refrigerator for 4 hours. Return to room temperature for 1 hour before cooking.

To make the salad, soak the cracked wheat in warm water for 30 minutes until the water has been absorbed and the grains have softened. Strain well to extract any excess water and transfer the wheat to a bowl. Add all the remaining ingredients, season to taste and set aside for 30 minutes to develop the flavours.

Thread the lamb onto large rosemary stalks or metal skewers. Cook on a preheated barbecue for 10 minutes, turning and basting from time to time. Leave to rest for 5 minutes, then serve with the salad.

500 g finely minced lean lamb

1 onion, grated

2 teaspoons ground cumin

1 teaspoon ground coriander

1 teaspoon paprika

½–1 teaspoon cayenne pepper

1 teaspoon sea salt

a small bunch of fresh flat leaf parsley, finely chopped

a small bunch of fresh coriander, finely chopped

leafy herb salad, to serve

flatbreads, to serve

Hot hoummus

225 g dried chickpeas, soaked overnight and cooked in plenty of water until tender, or a 410-g can cooked chickpeas, drained

50 ml olive oil

freshly squeezed juice of 1 lemon

1 teaspoon cumin seeds

2 tablespoons light tahini

4 tablespoons thick, strained natural yoghurt

sea salt and freshly ground black pepper

40 g butter

2 metal skewers with wide, flat blades

SERVES 4–6

cumin-flavoured lamb kebabs with hot hoummus

Typical fodder at the street grills or kebab houses, these kebabs are enjoyed throughout the Middle East and North Africa. To prepare them successfully, you will need large metal skewers with wide, flat blades to hold the meat.

Mix the minced lamb with the other ingredients and knead well. Pound the meat to a smooth consistency in a large mortar and pestle, or whizz in a food processor. Leave to sit for an hour to let the flavours mingle.

Meanwhile, make the hoummus. Preheat the oven to 200°C (400°F) Gas 6. In a food processor, whizz the chickpeas with the olive oil, lemon juice, cumin seeds, tahini and yoghurt. Season to taste, tip the mixture into an ovenproof dish, cover with foil and put in the preheated oven to warm through.

Wet your hands to make the meat mixture easier to handle. Mould portions of the mixture around the skewers, squeezing and flattening it, so it looks like the sheath to a sword.

Preheat the barbecue. Cook the kebabs for 4–5 minutes on each side. Quickly melt the butter in a saucepan or in the microwave and pour it over the hoummus. When the kebabs are cooked on both sides, slip the meat off the skewers, cut into bite-sized pieces and serve with the hot hoummus, with a leafy herb salad and flatbreads on the side.

lamb and porcini kebabs
with sage and parmesan

450 g tender lamb, from the leg or shoulder, cut into bite-sized chunks

2 tablespoons olive oil

freshly squeezed juice of 1–2 lemons

leaves from a bunch of fresh sage, finely chopped (reserve a few whole leaves)

2 garlic cloves, crushed

sea salt and freshly ground black pepper

4–8 fresh medium-sized porcini, cut into quarters or thickly sliced

To serve

truffle oil, to drizzle

Parmesan cheese shavings

grilled or toasted sourdough bread

4 long, thin metal skewers

SERVES 4

Rural feasts in Italy often involve grilling and roasting outdoors. One of the most exciting times is the mushroom season when entire villages hunt for wild mushrooms and gather together to cook them. These kebabs are prepared with fresh porcini, but you could substitute them with dried porcini reconstituted in water or field mushrooms.

Put the lamb pieces in a bowl and toss in the oil and lemon juice. Add the sage and garlic and season with salt and pepper. Cover and leave to marinate for about 2 hours.

Thread the lamb onto skewers adding a quarter, or slice, of porcini every so often with a sage leaf. Brush with any of the marinade left in the bowl. Prepare the barbecue. Cook the kebabs for 3–4 minutes on each side.

Serve immediately with a drizzle of truffle oil, Parmesan shavings and toasted sourdough bread, if liked.

500 g minced lean lamb

2 onions, finely chopped

1 fresh green chilli, finely chopped

4 garlic cloves, crushed

1 teaspoon paprika

1 teaspoon ground sumac
(see note on page 147)

leaves from a small bunch of fresh
flat leaf parsley, finely chopped

Sauce

2 tablespoons olive oil plus
a knob of butter

1 onion, finely chopped

2 garlic cloves, finely chopped

1 fresh green chilli, deseeded
and finely chopped

1 teaspoon sugar

400-g can chopped tomatoes

sea salt and freshly ground
black pepper

To serve

8 plum tomatoes

2 tablespoons butter

1 large pide or plain naan bread,
cut into pieces

1 teaspoon ground sumac

1 teaspoon dried oregano

225 g thick natural yoghurt

a bunch of fresh flat leaf parsley,
chopped

*1 large metal skewer with a wide,
flat blade, plus 1 long thin skewer*

SERVES 4

lamb shish kebab
with yoghurt and flatbread

There are variations of shish kebabs throughout the Middle East but this tasty Turkish version, designed to use up day-old 'pide' bread, is outstanding.

Put the minced lamb in a bowl. Add all the other kebab ingredients and knead well, until it resembles a smooth paste and is quite sticky. Cover and chill in the refrigerator for about 15 minutes.

To make the sauce, heat the oil and butter in a heavy-based saucepan. Add the onion, garlic and chilli, and stir until they begin to colour. Add the sugar and tomatoes and cook, uncovered, until quite thick. Season to taste. Keep warm.

Wet your hands to make the meat mixture easier to handle. Mould portions of the mixture around the large skewer, squeezing and flattening it, so it looks like the sheath to the sword. Thread the plum tomatoes onto the thin skewer.

Preheat the barbecue. Cook the kebab for 4–5 minutes on each side. Add the tomatoes to the grill and cook until charred and soft. While both are cooking, melt the butter in a heavy-based frying pan, add the pide pieces and toss until golden. Sprinkle with some of the sumac and oregano and arrange on a serving plate. Spoon some sauce and half the yoghurt on top.

When the kebab is cooked on both sides, slip the meat off the skewer, cut into pieces and arrange on top of the pide along with the tomatoes. Sprinkle with salt and the remaining sumac and oregano. Add more sauce and yoghurt and garnish with parsley.

top dogs

This hot dog recipe calls for good-quality pork sausages – rather than the more typical frankfurters usually associated with hot dogs – which are delicious combined with the caramelized onions and wholegrain mustard.

2 onions, cut into thin wedges

2–3 tablespoons extra virgin olive oil

1 tablespoon chopped fresh sage

sea salt and freshly ground black pepper

4 good-quality pork sausages, pricked

4 hot dog rolls

4 tablespoons wholegrain mustard

2 ripe tomatoes, sliced

SERVES 4

Put the onion wedges into a bowl, add the olive oil, sage and a little salt and pepper and mix well. Preheat the flat plate on the gas barbecue and cook the onions for 15–20 minutes, stirring occasionally until golden and tender. If you have a charcoal barbecue, cook the onions in a frying pan on top of the stove or on the barbecue. Keep hot.

Meanwhile, cook the sausages over hot coals for 10–12 minutes, turning frequently until charred and cooked through. Transfer to a plate and let rest briefly.

Cut the rolls almost in half, then put onto the grill rack and toast for a few minutes. Remove from the heat and spread with mustard. Fill with the tomatoes, sausages and onions.

750 g premium minced pork

2 garlic cloves, crushed

1 teaspoon grated fresh ginger

2 tablespoons chopped
fresh coriander

2 tablespoons cornflour

1 egg, lightly beaten

4 oval rolls

a handful of fresh herbs, such as
Thai or plain basil, coriander and
mint leaves

sea salt and freshly ground
black pepper

sunflower oil, for brushing

Satay sauce

4 tablespoons crunchy
peanut butter

2 tablespoons coconut cream

2 tablespoons freshly squeezed
lime juice

1 tablespoon sweet chilli sauce,
plus extra to serve

2 teaspoons light soy sauce

1 teaspoon soft brown sugar

*12 wooden or bamboo skewers,
soaked in water before use*

SERVES 4

spiced pork burger
with satay sauce

**This burger is inspired by some of the wonderful pork
skewers served in Thai restaurants, with their great
use of fresh herbs and satay sauce.**

Put the pork, garlic, ginger, coriander, cornflour, egg and salt and
pepper to taste in a bowl and work together with your hands until
evenly mixed. Divide into 12 portions and shape into small logs.
Cover and chill for 30 minutes.

Meanwhile, to make the satay sauce, put the peanut butter,
coconut cream, lime juice, chilli sauce, soy sauce and brown
sugar in a small saucepan and heat gently, stirring until mixed.
Simmer gently for 1–2 minutes until thickened. Set aside to cool.

Thread the patties onto the soaked skewers and brush with oil.
Barbecue or grill for 6–8 minutes, turning frequently until charred
on the outside and cooked through. Keep them warm.

To serve, split the rolls down the middle, open out and fill with
herbs. Remove the skewers from the pork patties and add the
patties to the rolls along with some satay sauce and sweet chilli
sauce. Serve hot.

aromatic pork burger in pita bread with chilli tomato chutney

150 g bread

5 tablespoons milk

800 g minced pork

2 eggs

a handful of fresh parsley, finely chopped

4 garlic cloves, crushed

1 teaspoon ground cinnamon

a large pinch of ground cloves

1 teaspoon ground turmeric

a large pinch of chilli powder

the seeds of 4 cardamom pods, crushed

1 teaspoon sea salt

freshly ground black pepper

olive oil, for brushing

Yoghurt dressing

300 ml natural set yoghurt

the seeds of 8 cardamom pods, crushed

a large pinch of sea salt

To serve

Chilli Tomato Chutney (page 35)

6 pita breads

150 g iceberg lettuce, shredded

SERVES 4–6

No barbecue is complete without burgers, but burgers don't necessarily have to mean junk food. Not only is it healthier to make your own, but fun too as you can experiment with herbs and spices to suit your own taste.

To make the yoghurt dressing, put the yoghurt and cardamom seeds in a small bowl, add the salt and mix well. Cover and refrigerate until required.

Soak the bread in the milk for 10–15 minutes until soft, then squeeze the bread with your hands until it is almost dry and put in a bowl. Add the minced pork, eggs, parsley, garlic, spices, salt and plenty of pepper. Mix well, cover and leave to stand for 1 hour.

Shape the meat mixture into 12 burgers. Cover and refrigerate until required.

When ready to cook, brush the burgers lightly with olive oil and cook them on a preheated hot barbecue for 20 minutes, turning them from time to time to avoid burning. Cut into one of the burgers to make sure it is cooked in the middle – if it is still pink, cook for an extra 5–10 minutes. Alternatively, cook the burgers in a frying pan over medium heat for 20 minutes, or put them in an oiled roasting tin and cook in a preheated oven at 180°C (350°F) Gas 4 for 20–30 minutes, turning from time to time. Transfer the burgers to a plate and spread each one with a spoonful of chilli tomato chutney.

Heat the pita breads on the barbecue or in the oven until just warm. Cut each one in half, open and fill with lettuce, yoghurt dressing and a burger, then serve.

Vietnamese pork balls

1 lemongrass stalk

500 g minced pork

125 g pork belly, minced

25 g breadcrumbs

6 kaffir lime leaves, very finely sliced

2 garlic cloves, crushed

2 cm fresh ginger, peeled and grated

1 fresh red chilli, deseeded and chopped

2 tablespoons Thai fish sauce

To serve

lettuce leaves

a handful of fresh herb leaves, such as mint, coriander and Thai basil

Sweet Chilli Sauce (page 20)

4 wooden or bamboo skewers, soaked in water before use

SERVES 4

Like many Vietnamese dishes, these delicious pork balls are served wrapped in a lettuce leaf with plenty of fresh herbs and Sweet Chilli Sauce.

Using a sharp knife, trim the lemongrass stalk to about 15 cm, then remove and discard the tough outer leaves. Chop the inner stalk very finely.

Put the minced pork and pork belly and breadcrumbs into a bowl, then add the lemongrass, lime leaves, garlic, ginger, chilli and fish sauce and mix well. Let marinate in the refrigerator for at least 1 hour.

Using your hands, shape the mixture into 20 small balls and carefully thread 5 onto each of the soaked wooden skewers. Preheat the barbecue, then brush the grill rack with oil. Cook the skewers over hot coals for 5–6 minutes, turning halfway through until cooked.

Serve the pork balls wrapped in the lettuce leaves with the herbs and sweet chilli sauce.

500 g pork fillet, cut into bite-sized cubes or strips

Marinade

4 shallots, peeled and chopped

4 garlic cloves, peeled

2–3 teaspoons curry powder

2 tablespoons dark soy sauce

2 tablespoons sesame or peanut oil

Pineapple sauce

4 shallots, peeled and chopped

2 garlic cloves, chopped

4 dried red chillies, soaked in warm water until soft, deseeded and chopped

1 lemongrass stalk, trimmed and chopped

25 g fresh ginger, peeled and chopped

2 tablespoons sesame or peanut oil

200 ml coconut milk

2 teaspoons tamarind paste (see note on page 160)

2 teaspoons sugar

1 small fresh pineapple, peeled, cored and cut into slices

sea salt

a packet of short wooden or bamboo skewers, soaked in water before use

SERVES 4

curried pork satay
with pineapple sauce

This spicy satay is popular in Malaysia and Singapore. A combination of Indian, Malay and Chinese traditions, it is best accompanied by a rice pilaf or chunks of bread.

To make the marinade, use a mortar and pestle, or a food processor, to pound the shallots and garlic to form a paste. Stir in the curry powder and soy sauce, and bind with the oil. Rub the marinade into the meat, making sure it is well coated. Cover and refrigerate for at least 2 hours.

In the meantime, prepare the sauce. Using a mortar and pestle, or a food processor, pound the shallots, garlic, chillies, lemongrass and ginger to form a paste. Heat the oil in a heavy-based pan and stir in the paste. Cook for 2–3 minutes until fragrant and beginning to colour, then stir in the coconut milk, tamarind and sugar. Bring the mixture to the boil, then reduce the heat and simmer for about 5 minutes. Season to taste and leave to cool. Using a mortar and pestle, or a food processor, crush 3 slices of the fresh pineapple and beat them into the sauce.

Preheat the barbecue. Thread the marinated meat onto the prepared skewers. Line them up over the hot charcoal or on the grill pan and place the remaining slices of pineapple beside them. Char the pineapple slices and chop them into chunks. Grill the meat until just cooked, roughly 2–3 minutes each side, and serve immediately with the charred pineapple chunks for spearing, and the sauce for dipping.

2 teaspoons peanut or sesame oil

4 shallots, finely chopped

2 garlic cloves, finely chopped

450 g minced pork

2 tablespoons Thai fish sauce

2 teaspoons Chinese five-spice powder

2 teaspoons sugar

2 handfuls of fresh white or brown breadcrumbs

sea salt and freshly ground black pepper

noodles, to serve

Sweet and sour sauce

2 teaspoons peanut oil

1 garlic clove, finely chopped

1 fresh red chilli, deseeded and finely chopped

2 tablespoons roasted peanuts, finely chopped

1 tablespoon Thai fish sauce

2 tablespoons rice wine vinegar

2 tablespoons hoisin sauce

4 tablespoons coconut milk

1–2 teaspoons sugar, to taste

a pinch of sea salt

a packet of short wooden or bamboo skewers, soaked in water before use

SERVES 4

pork kofta kebabs
with sweet and sour sauce

These Asian-style meatball kebabs are a delicious departure from the usual barbecue fare. They are best served with a hot, spicy dipping sauce and noodles. The sweet hoisin sauce is widely available in larger supermarkets and from Asian markets.

To make the sauce, heat the oil in a small wok or heavy-based frying pan. Stir in the garlic and chilli and, when they begin to colour, add the peanuts. Stir for a few minutes until the natural oil from the peanuts begins to weep. Add all the remaining ingredients (except the sugar and salt) along with 100 ml water. Let the mixture bubble up for 1 minute. Adjust the sweetness and seasoning to taste with sugar and some salt and set aside.

To make the meatballs, heat the oil in a wok or a heavy-based frying pan. Add the shallots and garlic – when they begin to brown, turn off the heat and leave to cool. Put the minced pork into a bowl, tip in the stir-fried shallot and garlic, fish sauce, five-spice powder and sugar and season with a little salt and lots of pepper. Using your hands, knead the mixture so it is well combined. Cover and chill in the refrigerator for 2–3 hours. Knead the mixture again then tip in the breadcrumbs. Knead well to bind. Divide the mixture into roughly 20 portions and roll into balls. Thread them onto the prepared skewers. Preheat the barbecue and cook the kebabs for 3–4 minutes on each side, turning them from time to time, until browned.

Reheat the sauce. Serve the kofta with noodles and the hot sweet and sour sauce on the side for dipping.

Although pork should not be served rare it is quite easy to overcook it, leaving the meat dry and tough. A good test is to pierce the meat with a skewer, leave it there for a second, remove it and carefully feel how hot it is – it should feel warm, not too hot or too cold, for the perfect result.

sage-rubbed pork chops

2 tablespoons chopped fresh sage

2 tablespoons wholegrain mustard

2 tablespoons extra virgin olive oil

4 large pork chops

sea salt and freshly ground black pepper

1 recipe Fresh Tomato Salsa (page 19), to serve

SERVES 4

Put the sage, mustard and olive oil into a bowl and mix well. Season with a little salt and pepper, then spread the mixture all over the chops. Let marinate in the refrigerator for 1 hour.

Preheat the barbecue, then cook the chops over hot coals for 2½–3 minutes on each side until browned and cooked through. Serve hot with the fresh tomato salsa.

2 garlic cloves, crushed

2 tablespoons sea salt

2 tablespoons ground cumin

1 teaspoon Tabasco sauce

1 teaspoon dried oregano

125 ml honey

4 tablespoons sherry vinegar

6 tablespoons olive oil

1 kg barbecue pork spareribs

Salsa

2 corn cobs, husks removed, brushed with corn oil

2 red peppers, quartered and deseeded

2 long red chillies, halved and deseeded

4 ripe red tomatoes, halved, deseeded and finely diced

1 red onion, chopped

2 garlic cloves, crushed

2 tablespoons chopped or torn fresh coriander

Dressing

½ teaspoon sugar

1 tablespoon corn oil

freshly squeezed juice of 1 lime

1 teaspoon salt, or to taste

freshly cracked black pepper

SERVES 4

barbecue spareribs
with Mexican salsa

The Mexican habit of grilling salsa ingredients first gives them a delicious, smoky, barbecue flavour. Toasted corn, chillies, peppers and even tomatoes all benefit from a bit of fire! Delicious served with the sweet ribs.

To make a marinade for the spareribs, put the garlic, salt, cumin, Tabasco, oregano, honey, vinegar and olive oil into a shallow dish and mix. Pat the ribs dry with kitchen paper, add them to the dish, then rub in the marinade. Cover and chill overnight.

Put the corn, pepper quarters and chilli halves onto a preheated barbecue or under the grill. Toast until the pepper and chilli skins and the corn are all lightly charred. Cool, then peel off the pepper and chilli skins (leaving a few charred bits behind) and slice the kernels off the corn cob. Put into a bowl, add the tomatoes, onion and garlic, then toss well.

To make the dressing for the salsa, put the sugar, corn oil, lime juice, salt and pepper into a bowl or jug, mix well, then pour over the vegetables and toss again. Cover and chill for at least 30 minutes. Before serving, stir through the chopped or torn coriander. Taste and add extra salt and freshly cracked black pepper if necessary.

When ready to cook, preheat the barbecue to medium, then add the ribs and cook on both sides for about 30 minutes until done. Baste from time to time with the marinade.

Cut the ribs into slices, each side of the bones, and arrange on 4 serving plates. Serve with the salsa beside or in a separate bowl. Have lots of napkins for mopping up, plus lots of cold beer.

Tex-Mex pork rack

2 racks barbecue pork spareribs, 500 g each

1 recipe Chilli Cornbread (page 212), to serve

Marinade

2 garlic cloves, crushed

2 tablespoons sea salt

2 tablespoons ground cumin

2 teaspoons chilli powder

1 teaspoon dried oregano

8 tablespoons maple syrup or golden syrup

4 tablespoons red wine vinegar

4 tablespoons olive oil

SERVES 4–6

Tex-Mex is a fusion of Mexican and Texan cuisines. It traditionally includes a lot of meat spiced up with hot ingredients such as chilli, and has even imported spices from other cuisines, such as cumin from Indian cooking, which is included here.

Wash the ribs and pat them dry with kitchen paper. Transfer to a shallow, non-metal dish.

Put all the marinade ingredients into a bowl, mix well, pour over the ribs, then work in well with your hands. Cover and let marinate overnight in the refrigerator.

The next day, return the ribs to room temperature for 1 hour, then cook on a preheated medium-hot barbecue for about 30 minutes, turning and basting frequently with the marinade juices. Cool a little, then serve with chilli cornbread.

poultry dishes

750 g skinless, boneless chicken breasts, minced

2 garlic cloves, crushed

1 tablespoon chopped fresh rosemary

freshly grated zest and juice of 1 unwaxed lemon

1 egg yolk

50 g dried breadcrumbs or matzo meal

1 medium aubergine

2 courgettes

4 slices focaccia

radicchio or rocket leaves

sea salt and freshly ground black pepper

olive oil, for brushing

Tapenade

125 g black olives, pitted

2 anchovies in oil, drained

1 garlic clove, crushed

2 tablespoons capers, rinsed

1 teaspoon Dijon mustard

4 tablespoons extra virgin olive oil

freshly ground black pepper

SERVES 4

open chicken burger
with grilled vegetables

This open-faced sandwich is full of the flavours of Mediterranean cooking, with char-grilled vegetables, focaccia bread and salty olive tapenade.

To make the tapenade, put the olives, anchovies, garlic, capers, mustard and oil in a food processor and blend to form a fairly smooth paste. Season to taste with pepper. Transfer to a dish, cover and store in the refrigerator for up to 5 days.

Put the chicken, garlic, rosemary, lemon zest and juice, egg yolk, breadcrumbs and some salt and pepper in a food processor and pulse until a smooth consistency. Transfer the mixture to a bowl, cover and chill for 30 minutes. Divide the mixture into 4 portions and shape into patties.

Cut the aubergine into 12 slices and the courgettes into 12 thin strips. Brush with olive oil and season with salt and pepper. Barbecue or grill the vegetables for 2–3 minutes on each side until charred and softened. Keep them warm.

Meanwhile, brush the chicken patties lightly with olive oil and barbecue for 5 minutes on each side until charred and cooked through. Keep them warm.

Toast the focaccia and top each slice with radicchio or rocket leaves, patties, grilled vegetables and some tapenade. Serve hot.

chicken steak burger
with Caesar dressing

4 small, skinless, boneless
chicken breasts

4 slices smoked back bacon

8 slices sourdough bread

1 cos lettuce heart,
leaves separated

25 g Parmesan cheese, pared
into shavings

sea salt and freshly ground
black pepper

olive oil, for brushing

Caesar dressing

4 tablespoons Mayonnaise
(page 199)

4 anchovies in oil, drained and
finely chopped

1 garlic clove, crushed

1 teaspoon Worcestershire sauce

1 teaspoon white wine vinegar

½ teaspoon Dijon mustard

SERVES 4

**The Caesar salad is as much an American icon as the
burger and here the two combine perfectly in a great
sourdough sandwich. You can add a poached egg to
the filling, if you like.**

Lay the chicken breast fillets flat on a chopping board and, using
a sharp knife, cut horizontally through the thickest part but don't
cut all the way through. Open the fillets out flat. Brush with olive
oil and season with salt and pepper.

Preheat a barbecue and cook the chicken fillets for 3–4 minutes
on each side until cooked through. Keep them warm. Cook the
bacon on the barbecue for 2–3 minutes until cooked to your
liking. Keep it warm. Toast the sourdough over the coals until
lightly charred.

Meanwhile, to make the dressing, put the mayonnaise,
anchovies, garlic, Worcestershire sauce, vinegar and mustard
in a bowl and beat well. Add salt and pepper to taste.

Spread each slice of sourdough with a little Caesar dressing
and top half of them with lettuce, chicken, bacon and Parmesan
shavings. Finish with a second slice of sourdough and serve hot.

'Panini' is the Italian word for little sandwiches, usually toasted. Instead of bread, this recipe uses a chicken breast fillet, stuffed with basil and mozzarella and barbecued until melted, gooey and delicious!

chicken 'panini'
with mozzarella and salsa rossa

250 g mozzarella cheese, cut into 8 thick slices

4 large, skinless, boneless chicken breasts

8 large basil leaves, plus extra to serve

2 garlic cloves, sliced thinly

1 tablespoon extra virgin olive oil

sea salt and freshly ground black pepper

1 recipe Salsa Rossa (see page 151), to serve

SERVES 4

Put the chicken breasts onto a board and, using a sharp knife, cut horizontally through the thickness without cutting all the way through. Open out flat and season the insides with a little salt and pepper. Put 2 basil leaves, a few garlic slices and 2 slices of cheese into each breast, then fold back over, pressing firmly together. Secure with cocktail sticks.

Brush the parcels with a little oil and cook on a preheated barbecue or stove-top grill pan for about 8 minutes on each side until the cheese is beginning to ooze at the sides. Serve hot with the salsa rossa and sprinkle with a few basil leaves.

whole chicken roasted on the barbecue

1.5 kg whole chicken

1 lemon, halved

4 garlic cloves, peeled

a small bunch of fresh thyme

extra virgin olive oil

sea salt and freshly ground black pepper

a barbecue with a lid

SERVES 4–6

Cooking with the lid on your barbecue creates the same effect as cooking in a conventional oven. If you don't have a barbecue with a lid, you can cut the chicken in half and cook on the grill for about 15 minutes on each side.

Wash the chicken thoroughly under cold running water and pat dry with kitchen paper.

Rub the chicken all over with the halved lemon, then put the lemon halves inside the body cavity with the garlic, cloves and thyme. Rub a little olive oil into the skin and season liberally with salt and pepper.

Preheat the barbecue and when the coals are ready, rake them into two piles and carefully place a drip tray in the middle. Remove the grill rack and brush or spray it with oil. Return it to the barbecue and put the chicken on the rack above the drip tray. Cover with the lid, then cook over medium hot coals for 1 hour or until the skin is golden, the flesh is cooked through and the juices run clear when the thickest part of the meat is pierced with a skewer. If any bloody juices appear, cook for a little longer.

Let the chicken rest for 10 minutes before serving.

barbecued Mexican-style poussins

Spatchcocked poussins are ideally suited to barbecue cooking, as the process of opening them out flat ensures quick and even cooking. The marinade ingredients have a Mexican flavour and work particularly well accompanied by the creamy corn salsa on page 23.

4 poussins

1 recipe Creamy Corn Salsa (page 23), to serve

Mexican marinade

4 jalapeño chillies

8 garlic cloves, peeled

4 tablespoons freshly squeezed orange juice

2 tablespoons freshly squeezed lime juice

1 tablespoon ground cumin

1 tablespoon dried oregano or thyme

2 teaspoons sea salt

6 tablespoons olive oil

1 tablespoon maple syrup or clear honey

8 wooden or bamboo skewers, soaked in water before use

SERVES 4

To spatchcock the poussins, turn them breast side down and, using poultry shears or sturdy scissors, cut down each side of the backbone and discard it. Turn the birds over and open them out flat, pressing down hard on the breastbone. Thread 2 skewers diagonally through each poussin from the wings to the thigh bones.

To make the marinade, skewer the chillies and garlic together and cook on a preheated medium-hot barbecue or under a grill for 10 minutes, turning frequently, until evenly browned. Scrape off and discard the skins from the chillies and chop the flesh coarsely. Put the flesh and seeds into a food processor, add the garlic and all the remaining marinade ingredients and blend to a purée.

Pour the marinade over the poussins and let marinate in the refrigerator overnight. Return them to room temperature for 1 hour before cooking

When ready to cook, remove the birds from their marinade and barbecue over medium-hot preheated coals for 12 minutes on each side, basting occasionally. Remove from the heat, let rest for 5 minutes, then serve with the creamy corn salsa.

jerk chicken wings
with avocado salsa

12 chicken wings

2 tablespoons extra virgin olive oil

1 tablespoon jerk seasoning powder or 2 tablespoons paste

freshly squeezed juice of ½ lemon

1 teaspoon sea salt

Avocado salsa

1 large ripe avocado

2 ripe tomatoes, peeled, deseeded and chopped

1 garlic clove, crushed

1 small red chilli, deseeded and chopped

freshly squeezed juice of ½ lemon

2 tablespoons chopped fresh coriander

1 tablespoon extra virgin olive oil

sea salt and freshly ground black pepper

SERVES 4

Jerk seasoning is Jamaica's popular spice mix, used to spark up meat, poultry and fish. It is a combination of allspice, cinnamon, chilli, nutmeg, thyme and sugar and is widely available in powder or paste form from larger supermarkets and specialist food stores.

Put the chicken wings in a ceramic dish. Mix the oil, jerk seasoning, lemon juice and salt in a bowl, pour over the wings and stir well until evenly coated. Cover and let marinate overnight in the refrigerator.

The next day cook the wings on the barbecue for 5–6 minutes each side, basting them occasionally with any remaining marinade until they are charred and tender.

Meanwhile, to make the salsa, put all the ingredients into a bowl, mix well and season to taste. Serve the wings with the salsa.

Note If you don't have any jerk seasoning to hand, try another spice mix or spice paste instead. Just remember, jerk is very fiery indeed, so you need a spicy one.

char-grilled chicken breast
with mixed leaves and balsamic dressing

4 fresh boneless chicken breasts, about 1 kg

150 g mixed salad leaves, such as rocket, watercress, lambs' lettuce, radicchio or baby spinach, to serve

1 recipe Sesame Sweet Potato Packets (see page 188), to serve

Marinade

2 teaspoons Chinese five-spice powder

1 teaspoon ground ginger

2 tablespoons balsamic vinegar

1 tablespoon extra virgin olive oil

1 teaspoon sea salt

freshly ground black pepper

Balsamic dressing

4 tablespoons extra virgin olive oil

2 tablespoons balsamic vinegar

1 teaspoon mustard powder

1 tablespoon freshly squeezed lemon juice

2 teaspoons sugar

sea salt and freshly ground black pepper

a ridged stove-top grill pan

SERVES 4

The chicken in this recipe is marinaded in Chinese five-spice powder. It is distinctive and aromatic, without being overpowering, and it lends itself to marinades of all kinds.

Lay a piece of clingfilm on a chopping board, put a chicken breast in the middle and flatten it with the palms of your hands. Cover it with a second piece of clingfilm, beat it flat with a meat cleaver, then remove the clingfilm. Repeat with the remaining chicken breasts.

To make the marinade, put the five-spice powder, ginger, vinegar, olive oil and salt in a small bowl, season with black pepper and mix well. Spoon this over both sides of the chicken breasts, piling them on a plate as you go. Cover and leave to stand for 1–24 hours to suit. (If marinating for more than 1 hour, put the chicken in the refrigerator.)

To make the balsamic dressing, put the olive oil, vinegar, mustard powder, lemon juice and sugar in a jar, then add salt and pepper to taste, put the lid on and shake well.

When ready to cook, put the chicken on a preheated hot ridged stove-top grill pan on top of a preheated hot barbecue and cook on both sides until charred, about 10 minutes in total, lifting the corners from time to time to check that it is not burning. To make sure the chicken is cooked, cut into the thickest part with a sharp knife – if it is still pink, cook for a few more minutes.

Cover a large serving platter with the salad leaves. Arrange the cooked chicken breasts on top and drizzle the dressing over the chicken and the salad. Serve immediately with sesame sweet potato packets.

This delicious concoction of olives, lemons, fresh marjoram and succulent chicken makes an ideal main course for a barbecue party. Serve with a selection of salads, such as tomato and basil.

olive-infused chicken
with charred lemons

1.5 kg whole chicken

75 g pitted black olives

4 tablespoons extra virgin olive oil

1 teaspoon sea salt

2 tablespoons chopped
fresh marjoram

freshly squeezed juice of 1 lemon
plus 2 lemons, halved

freshly ground black pepper

SERVES 4

To prepare the chicken, put it onto a board with the back facing upwards and, using kitchen scissors, cut along each side of the backbone and remove it completely. Using your fingers, gently ease the skin away from the flesh, taking care not to tear the skin, then put the chicken into a large, shallow dish. Put the olives, olive oil, salt, marjoram and lemon juice into a separate bowl and mix well, then pour over the chicken and push as many of the olives as possible up between the skin and flesh of the chicken. Let marinate in the refrigerator for 2 hours.

Preheat the barbecue, then cook the chicken cut side down over medium hot coals for 15 minutes. Using tongs, turn the chicken over and cook for a further 10 minutes until the skin is charred, the flesh is cooked through and the juices run clear when the thickest part of the meat is pierced with a skewer. While the chicken is cooking, add the halved lemons to the grill and cook for about 10–15 minutes until charred and tender on all sides.

Let the chicken rest for 10 minutes before cutting into 4 pieces and serving with the lemons.

harissa chicken kebabs
with oranges and preserved lemon

16–20 chicken wings

4 oranges (blood oranges if available), cut into quarters

about 30 g icing sugar

½ a preserved lemon*, finely shredded or chopped

a small bunch of fresh coriander, chopped

Marinade

4 tablespoons harissa paste

2 tablespoons olive oil

sea salt

4 long, thin metal skewers

SERVES 4

With a taste of North Africa, this recipe is quick and easy and best eaten with fingers. The oranges are there to suck on after an explosion of fire on the tongue. They can be cooked separately, or threaded alternately on metal skewers.

Mix the harissa with the olive oil to form a looser paste and add a little salt. Brush the oily mixture over the chicken wings, so that they're well coated. Leave to marinate for 2 hours.

Thread the marinated chicken wings onto the skewers. Preheat the barbecue. Cook on both sides for about 5 minutes. Once the wings begin to cook, dip the orange quarters lightly in icing sugar, thread them onto skewers and grill them for a few minutes, checking that they are slightly charred but not burnt.

Serve the chicken wings and oranges together and scatter the preserved lemon and coriander over the top.

*Note Preserved lemons are used extensively in North African cooking and are whole lemons packed in jars with salt. The interesting thing is that you eat only the rind, which contains the essential flavour of the lemon. They are available from supermarkets and online retailers.

500 g skinless, boneless chicken breasts

Marinade

250 ml natural yoghurt

2 tablespoons extra virgin olive oil

2 garlic cloves, crushed

grated zest and freshly squeezed juice of 1 unwaxed lemon

1–2 teaspoons chilli powder

1 tablespoon chopped fresh coriander

sea salt and freshly ground black pepper

a packet of wooden or bamboo skewers, soaked in water before use

SERVES 4

Yoghurt crusted chicken threaded onto skewers makes ideal finger food for casual barbecues. The yoghurt tenderizes the chicken and helps the lemon soak into the meat – and becomes delicious and slightly crunchy when cooked over coals.

chicken lemon skewers

Cut the chicken fillets lengthways into 2 mm thick strips and put into a shallow ceramic dish.

Put all the marinade ingredients into a bowl, stir well and pour over the chicken, turn to coat, cover and let marinate in the refrigerator overnight.

The next day, thread the chicken onto the prepared skewers, zigzagging the meat back and forth as you go.

Cook on a preheated barbecue for 3–4 minutes on each side until charred and tender. Let cool slightly before serving.

1 kg skinless, boneless chicken breasts, cut into bite-sized pieces

2 tablespoons ghee or butter, melted

Marinade

3 fresh red or green chillies, deseeded and chopped

2–3 garlic cloves, chopped

25 g fresh ginger, peeled and chopped

2 tablespoons double cream

3 tablespoons vegetable oil

1 tablespoon paprika

2 teaspoons ground cumin

2 teaspoons ground cardamom

1 teaspoon ground cloves

1 teaspoon sea salt

To serve

crispy poppadoms

tomato and cucumber salad

limes wedges (optional)

4–6 long, thin metal skewers

SERVES 4–6

chicken tandoori kebabs

As the name of this dish denotes, it should be cooked in a tandoori oven but, as most of us don't have such a wonderful invention at home, a barbecue is a great substitute. Some Indian and African cooks add red food dye to the marinade to obtain the reddish colouring associated with tandoori dishes.

To prepare the marinade, use a mortar and pestle, or a food processor, to mince the chillies, garlic and ginger to a paste. Beat in the cream and oil with 3–4 tablespoons water to form a smooth mixture. Beat in the dried spices.

Place the chicken pieces in a bowl and rub with the marinade until thoroughly coated. Cover and chill in the refrigerator for about 48 hours. Lift the chicken pieces out of the marinade and thread them onto the skewers. Prepare the barbecue. Brush the chicken with the melted ghee and grill for 3–4 minutes on each side. Serve with crispy poppadoms, a salad of finely diced tomato, cucumber and onion with fresh coriander, and wedges of lime for squeezing, if liked.

spicy chicken kebabs
with ground almonds

700 g skinless, boneless chicken breasts, cut into bite-sized pieces

freshly squeezed juice of 1 lemon

1 teaspoon sea salt

1–2 tablespoons peanut or sunflower oil

1 onion, halved and sliced

25 g fresh ginger, peeled and finely grated

2 garlic cloves, crushed

2–3 tablespoons ground almonds

1–2 teaspoons garam masala

125 ml thick double cream

To serve

1–2 tablespoons butter

2–3 tablespoons blanched, flaked almonds

a small bunch of fresh flat leaf parsley, finely chopped

warmed flatbreads

4 long, thin metal skewers

SERVES 4

In India, Turkey and North Africa, nuts are often used in recipes. Sometimes they are hidden in the minced meat of a kofta (meatball), or they form a coating on the meat. In this dish, the combination of ground almonds and browned onions in the marinade gives the meat a sweet, rich flavour.

First, toss the chicken pieces in the lemon juice and salt to blanch them. Put aside for 15 minutes.

Meanwhile, heat the oil in a frying pan. Add the onion and cook until golden brown and crisp. Remove the onion from the oil and spread it out on a sheet of kitchen paper to drain and cool. Reserve the oil in the frying pan.

Using a mortar and pestle, or a food processor, pound the onions to a paste and beat in the ginger and garlic. Add the almonds and garam masala and bind with the cream. Tip the almond and onion mixture over the chicken and mix well. Cover and leave in the refrigerator to marinate for about 6 hours.

Thread the chicken onto the skewers and brush them with the reserved onion oil. Prepare the barbecue. Cook the kebabs for 3–4 minutes on each side, until the chicken is nicely browned. Quickly melt the butter in a pan and stir in the flaked almonds until golden. Toss in the parsley and spoon the mixture over the grilled chicken. Serve hot with warmed flatbreads, if liked.

500 g skinless, boneless chicken breasts

2 tablespoons extra virgin olive oil

freshly squeezed juice of
1 large lemon

1 tablespoon chopped fresh thyme leaves

2 garlic cloves, crushed

1 teaspoon ground turmeric

1 teaspoon ground cinnamon

½ teaspoon ground allspice

½ teaspoon salt

¼ teaspoon ground cayenne pepper

lemon wedges, to serve

natural yoghurt, to serve

8 wooden or bamboo skewers, soaked in water before use

SERVES 4

chicken kebabs Moroccan-style

These delicious kebabs are wondrously flavoured with scented North African spices. Serve them as snacks with a yoghurt dip and flatbread, or with traditional Moroccan couscous as a main meal at a barbecue party.

Cut the chicken lengthways into 3 mm strips and put into a shallow ceramic dish. Put the oil, lemon juice, thyme, garlic, turmeric, cinnamon, allspice, salt and cayenne into a jug, mix well, then pour over the chicken.

Cover and marinate overnight in the refrigerator.

The next day, return to room temperature for 1 hour. Thread the strips onto skewers, zigzagging back and forth. Cook on a preheated barbecue for 3–4 minutes on each side until charred and cooked through. Serve with lemon wedges and yoghurt.

700 g duck breasts or boned thighs, sliced into thin, bite-sized strips

1–2 tablespoons peanut or coconut oil, for brushing

1 small pineapple, peeled, cored and sliced

Chinese plum sauce, to serve

Marinade

2–3 tablespoons light soy sauce

freshly squeezed juice of 1 lime

1–2 teaspoons sugar

1–2 garlic cloves, crushed

25 g fresh ginger, peeled and grated

1 small onion, grated

1–2 teaspoons ground coriander

1 teaspoon sea salt

a packet of wooden or bamboo skewers, soaked in water before use

SERVES 4

duck satay with grilled pineapple and plum sauce

Chicken satays are popular throughout Southeast Asia but in Vietnam, Cambodia and China, duck satays are common too. Duck is often served in the Chinese tradition of sweet and sour with a fruity sauce. You can buy ready-made bottled plum sauce in Chinese markets and most supermarkets.

To make the marinade, put the soy sauce and lime juice in a bowl with the sugar and mix until it dissolves. Add the garlic, ginger and grated onion and stir in the coriander and salt.

Place the strips of duck in a bowl and pour over the marinade. Toss well, cover and chill in the refrigerator for at least 4 hours. Thread the duck strips onto the skewers and brush them with oil.

Prepare the barbecue. Cook the satays for 3–4 minutes on each side, until the duck is nicely browned. Grill the slices of pineapple at the same time. When browned, cut them into bite-sized pieces and serve with the duck. Drizzle with the plum sauce to serve.

duck yakitori

6 tablespoons Japanese
soy sauce

3 tablespoons sake

2 tablespoons caster sugar

4 small duck breast fillets, about
150 g each, skinned

soba noodles, cooked according
to the packet instructions, then
drained and chilled, to serve

Cucumber salad

2 tablespoons rice vinegar

2 tablespoons caster sugar

½ cucumber, about 20 cm,
finely sliced

1 red chilli, deseeded and
chopped

*8 wooden or bamboo skewers,
soaked in water before use*

SERVES 4

Yakitori is a Japanese-style kebab, which is usually cooked over coals and so is perfect for barbecues. The rich sauce in this recipe copes perfectly with the gamey taste of duck and tenderizes the flesh beautifully.

Put the soy sauce, sake and sugar into a small saucepan and heat gently to dissolve the sugar. Cool completely.

Cut the duck lengthways into 3 mm strips and put into a shallow dish. Pour over the soy sauce mixture and marinate in the refrigerator for 2–4 hours or overnight.

Just before cooking the duck, prepare the salad. Put the vinegar, sugar and 2 tablespoons water into a small saucepan, heat to dissolve the sugar, then let cool. Stir in the cucumber and chilli and set aside.

Thread the duck strips onto skewers, zigzagging back and forth. Cook on a preheated barbecue for 2 minutes on each side until cooked through. Serve with chilled soba noodles and the cucumber salad.

fish & seafood

750 g swordfish steak

extra virgin olive oil

½ recipe Moroccan Rub (page 16)

24 large bay leaves, soaked in cold water for 1 hour

2 lemons, cut into 24 chunks

freshly squeezed lemon juice, to serve

Couscous

250 g couscous

300 ml boiling water

50 g freshly grated Parmesan cheese

50 g butter, melted

1 tablespoon chopped fresh thyme

sea salt and freshly ground black pepper

8 wooden or bamboo skewers, soaked in water before use

SERVES 4

Chunks of swordfish coated in a spicy rub, then barbecued on skewers and served with freshly cooked couscous, make the perfect al fresco lunch. Chicken would also work well, if you prefer.

Moroccan fish skewers

with couscous

Using a sharp knife, cut the swordfish into 32 cubes and put into a shallow ceramic dish. Add a sprinkle of olive oil and the Moroccan rub, toss well until the fish is evenly coated. Let marinate in the refrigerator for 1 hour.

About 10 minutes before cooking the fish, put the couscous into a sieve and rinse under cold running water to moisten all the grains, then put into a steamer and steam for 10 minutes or until the grains have softened. Transfer the couscous to a warmed serving dish and immediately stir in the Parmesan cheese, melted butter, thyme and seasonings. Keep the couscous warm.

Meanwhile, preheat the barbecue. Thread the fish, bay leaves and chunks of lemon onto the prepared skewers and cook over hot coals for 3–4 minutes, turning halfway through until cooked. Serve the skewers on a bed of couscous, sprinkled with olive oil and lemon juice.

Note One hour is sufficient to flavour the fish with the spice rub, any longer and the flavours of the rub can become overpowering.

2 unwaxed lemons

250 ml extra virgin olive oil

1 tablespoon dried oregano

2 garlic cloves, finely chopped

2 tablespoons chopped fresh flat leaf parsley

6 bream or snapper, about 350 g each, well cleaned and scaled

sea salt and freshly ground black pepper

SERVES 6

barbecued fish
bathed in oregano and lemon

This recipe for the classic summer dish of char-grilled fish with lemon, oregano and garlic, uses bream, but you could use other small fish such as snapper, red mullet or even trout if you prefer.

Grate the zest of 1 lemon into a small bowl and squeeze in the juice. Add 225 ml of the oil, the oregano, garlic, parsley, salt and pepper. Leave to infuse for at least 1 hour.

Wash and dry the fish inside and out. Using a sharp knife, cut several slashes into each side. Squeeze the juice from the remaining lemon into a bowl, add the remaining 4 tablespoons of oil, salt and pepper and rub the mixture all over the fish.

Heat the flat plate of your barbecue for 10 minutes, add the fish and cook for 3–4 minutes on each side until charred and cooked through. Alternatively, use a large, heavy-based frying pan or stove-top grill pan. Transfer to a large, warm platter, pour over the lemon dressing and let rest for 5 minutes before serving.

red snapper
with parsley salad

4 red snapper, cleaned and well scaled, about 350 g each

1 recipe Herb, Lemon and Garlic Marinade (page 15)

Parsley salad

50 g raisins

2 tablespoons verjuice* or white grape juice

leaves from a large bunch of fresh parsley

25 g pine nuts, toasted

50 g feta cheese, crumbled

3 tablespoons extra virgin olive oil

2 teaspoons balsamic vinegar

sea salt and freshly ground black pepper

SERVES 4

Even if the snapper has already been scaled by the fishmonger, go over it again to remove any stray scales – they are huge! A fish grilling basket could also be useful for cooking this fish.

Using a sharp knife, cut several slashes into each side of the fish. Put into a shallow ceramic dish and add the marinade. Let marinate in the refrigerator for 4 hours, but return to room temperature for 1 hour before cooking.

Just before cooking the fish, make the salad. Put the raisins into a bowl, add the verjuice and let soak for 15 minutes. Drain and set the liquid aside. Put the parsley, pine nuts, soaked raisins and feta into a bowl. Put the olive oil, vinegar and reserved raisin liquid into a separate bowl and mix well. Pour over the salad and toss until the leaves are well coated. Season with salt and pepper.

Preheat the barbecue, then cook the fish over hot coals for 4–5 minutes on each side, let rest briefly and serve with the salad.

*Note Verjuice, which is used in the salad dressing, is produced from the juice of unripe grapes. It is available from Italian delicatessens. If you can't find it, use white grape juice instead.

1 rounded teaspoon fennel seeds

1 rounded teaspoon dried oregano

1 teaspoon cumin seeds

1 teaspoon sea salt

1 teaspoon green or black peppercorns

¼ teaspoon crushed chillies

6 small seabass, gutted and scaled (ask the fishmonger or assistant at the fish counter to do this for you)

extra virgin olive oil spray

3 unwaxed lemons

a few bay leaves

4 baby fennel bulbs

350 g cherry tomatoes

wedges of lemon, to serve

6 wooden or bamboo skewers, soaked in water before use

SERVES 6

Sicilian-spiced seabass with grilled tomatoes and baby fennel

A simple but impressive dish that is easy to cook on the barbecue. If whole fish don't appeal, you could make this recipe with tuna or swordfish steaks.

Heat a gas barbecue or light a charcoal barbecue.

Crush the fennel seeds, oregano, cumin seeds, salt, peppercorns and chilli together thoroughly in a mortar with a pestle. Make 3 slashes in each side of the fish with a sharp knife. Spray the fish with olive oil and rub the pounded spices over the fish and into the slits. Cut 2 of the lemons in half vertically, then cut 1½ into thin slices. Cut or tear the bay leaves into halves or thirds. Place half a slice of lemon and a piece of bay leaf in each slit.

Cut each fennel bulb in quarters lengthways and thread the cherry tomatoes onto the skewers. Spray the fish, fennel and tomatoes with oil and grill over medium heat until charred, turning them halfway through, removing them as they are cooked. Serve with wedges of lemon.

barbecued salmon steaks
with basil and parmesan butter

Flavoured butters help to keep the fish deliciously moist, but be sure to watch the steaks carefully while cooking as they can easily overcook. Brushing the bars of the grill with a little oil will prevent the salmon from sticking.

6 fresh salmon steaks, cut about 2 cm thick, 1.5 kg total weight

Basil and Parmesan butter

175 g unsalted butter

25 g freshly grated Parmesan cheese

1 teaspoon balsamic or sherry vinegar

25 g fresh basil leaves, sliced

freshly ground black pepper

Marinade

1 large garlic clove, crushed

150 ml light olive oil

2 tablespoons balsamic or sherry vinegar

1–2 sprigs of fresh thyme, crushed

SERVES 6

To make the basil and Parmesan butter, beat the butter until soft. Gradually beat in the grated Parmesan, vinegar, basil leaves and ground black pepper to taste. Scoop onto a piece of wet greaseproof paper and roll into a cylinder. Wrap in clingfilm and refrigerate (or freeze) for at least 1 hour, or until firm.

Put the marinade ingredients in a wide, shallow dish, mix well, then add the salmon steaks and turn to coat well. Cover and let marinate for 20–30 minutes. Lift the steaks from the marinade and pat dry with kitchen paper.

Heat a barbecue until the coals are medium hot and white (no longer red). Lightly oil the grill bars, add the salmon and barbecue for about 3 minutes on each side until crisp and brown on the outside and just opaque all the way through – overcooked salmon is dry, so be careful to cook it properly. Serve the salmon steaks covered with slices of the chilled butter melting on top.

Note If using other herbs, such as parsley, tarragon or marjoram, always use fresh: dried herbs are not very successful.

2 fresh tail-end salmon fillets, 400 g each, skin on

sea salt and freshly ground black pepper

Mustard marinade

3 tablespoons Dijon mustard

2 tablespoons soy sauce

1 large garlic clove, crushed

1 tablespoon chopped fresh ginger

3 tablespoons chopped fresh tarragon

kitchen string

SERVES 6–8

mustard-barbecued salmon tail

A fantastic way to roast or barbecue a gigot of salmon. If you have a barbecue with a lid, the salmon will take a shorter time to cook – just don't keep lifting the lid.

To make the marinade, mix the mustard, soy, garlic, ginger and tarragon in a bowl.

Put one salmon fillet skin-side down on a board and spread liberally with the mustard mix. Season well. Arrange the other fillet on top and tie up in 3 or 4 places with string. Cover and refrigerate for about 2 hours for the flavours to permeate the flesh. Return to room temperature before cooking.

When ready to cook, preheat a barbecue until the coals are white and no longer red. Brush the salmon with a little oil and barbecue over medium hot coals for about 15 minutes per side, or until the fish is opaque all the way through.

Serve immediately by untying the string and lifting off the top fillet. Lift the salmon off the skin to serve.

Note There are heavy foil trays available: if you 'roast' the salmon on one of these, it will catch the delicious juices.

A great way to prepare whole salmon is to remove the central bone from the fish, then tie the two fillets back together. If your filleting skills are limited, just ask your friendly fishmonger to fillet the whole fish for you.

whole salmon stuffed with herbs

2 kg whole salmon, filleted

125 g butter, softened

25 g chopped, fresh soft-leaf mixed herbs, such as basil, chives, mint, parsley and tarragon

grated zest of 1 unwaxed lemon

1 garlic clove, crushed

sea salt and freshly ground black pepper

olive oil, for brushing

kitchen string

SERVES 8

Put the salmon fillets flat onto a board, flesh side up. Carefully pull out any remaining bones with tweezers.

Put the butter, herbs, lemon zest, garlic and plenty of pepper into a small bowl and beat well. Spread the mixture over one of the salmon fillets and put the second on the top, arranging them top to tail.

Using kitchen string, tie the fish together at 2.5 cm intervals. Brush with a little oil, sprinkle with salt and freshly ground black pepper and cook on the flat plate of a barbecue for 10 minutes on each side. Let rest for a further 10 minutes. Remove the string and serve the fish cut into portions.

stuffed char-grilled sardines

4 good-sized fresh sardines

2 tablespoons olive oil

4–6 spring onions, finely sliced

2–3 garlic cloves, crushed

1 teaspoon cumin seeds, crushed

1 teaspoon ground sumac
(see note on page 147)

1 tablespoon pine nuts

1 tablespoon currants, soaked
in warm water for 15 minutes
and drained

a small bunch of fresh flat leaf
parsley, finely chopped

sea salt and freshly ground
black pepper

Basting

3 tablespoons olive oil

freshly squeezed juice of 1 lemon

1–2 teaspoons ground sumac

*a packet of wooden or bamboo
skewers, soaked in water
before use*

SERVES 4

This dish is best made with good-sized plump, fresh sardines, which are slit from head to tail with the back bone removed. Full of Mediterranean flavours, this is a great recipe for outdoor cooking on the barbecue while enjoying the summer sunshine.

To prepare the sardines, remove the bone, gently massage the area around it to loosen it. Using your fingers, carefully prise out the bone, snapping it off at each end, while keeping the fish intact. Rinse the fish and pat it dry before stuffing.

Heat the oil in a heavy-based pan and stir in the spring onions until soft. Add the garlic, cumin and sumac. Stir in the pine nuts and pre-soaked currants, and fry until the pine nuts begin to turn golden. Toss in the parsley and season with salt and pepper. Leave to cool.

Place the sardines on a flat surface and spread the filling inside each one. When stuffed, seal the fish by threading the skewers through the soft belly flaps.

Mix together the olive oil, lemon juice and sumac and brush some of it over the sardines. Prepare a charcoal or conventional grill. Cook the stuffed fish for 2–3 minutes on each side, basting them with the rest of the olive oil mixture. Serve immediately.

swordfish kebabs
with oranges and sumac

500 g boned swordfish, cut into bite-sized chunks

2 oranges, cut into wedges

a handful of fresh bay leaves

2–3 teaspoons ground sumac*

Marinade

1 onion, grated

1–2 garlic cloves, crushed

freshly squeezed juice of ½ a lemon

2–3 tablespoons olive oil

1–2 teaspoons tomato purée

sea salt and freshly ground black pepper

4 metal skewers or 4–6 wooden skewers, soaked in water before use

SERVES 4

Any firm-fleshed fish, such as tuna, trout, salmon, monkfish and sea bass, can be used for these mighty Middle Eastern kebabs. Make life easy and buy the swordfish ready boned from the fishmonger. Exotic sumac adds a lemony tang.

In a shallow bowl, mix together the ingredients for the marinade. Toss the chunks of swordfish in the marinade and set aside to marinate for 30 minutes.

Thread the marinated fish onto the skewers, alternating it with the orange segments and the occasional bay leaf. If there is any marinade left, brush it over the kebabs.

Prepare the barbecue. Cook the kebabs for 2–3 minutes on each side, until the fish is nicely browned. Sprinkle the kebabs with sumac and serve.

*Note Sumac is an increasingly popular spice. It grows wild, but is also cultivated in Italy, Sicily and throughout the Middle East. It is widely used in Lebanese, Syrian, Turkish and Iranian cooking. The red berries have an astringent quality, with a pleasing sour-fruit flavour. They are used whole, but ground sumac is available from Middle Eastern grocers or specialist online retailers.

Swordfish is delicious char-grilled, but it is easy to overcook, and will become tough, so follow the timings below and err on the side of caution – you can always put the fish back on the barbecue for a moment or two longer if necessary.

seared swordfish with new potatoes, beans and olives

4 swordfish steaks, 200 g each

1 tablespoon extra virgin olive oil

500 g new potatoes, halved if large

200 g green beans, trimmed

50 g pitted black or green olives, chopped

balsamic vinegar (optional), to serve

Dressing

6 tablespoons extra virgin olive oil

2 tablespoons freshly squeezed lemon juice

½ teaspoon caster sugar

1 tablespoon chopped fresh chives

sea salt and freshly ground black pepper

SERVES 4

Brush the swordfish steaks with the oil, season with salt and pepper and set aside.

To make the dressing, put the oil into a bowl, add the lemon juice, sugar, chives and salt and pepper, beat well and set aside.

Cook the potatoes in a saucepan of lightly salted boiling water for 10 minutes, add the beans and cook for a further 3–4 minutes or until the potatoes and beans are just tender. Drain well, add the olives and half the dressing and toss well.

Cook the swordfish steaks on a preheated barbecue for about 1½ minutes on each side. Let rest in a warm oven for 5 minutes, then serve with the warm potato salad, sprinkled with the remaining dressing and a splash of balsamic vinegar, if liked.

peppered tuna steak
with salsa rossa

6 tablespoons mixed peppercorns, coarsely crushed

6 tuna steaks, 200 g each

1 tablespoon extra virgin olive oil, for brushing

mixed leaf salad, to serve

Salsa rossa

1 large red pepper

1 tablespoon extra virgin olive oil

2 garlic cloves, crushed

2 large ripe tomatoes, peeled and roughly chopped

a small pinch of dried chilli flakes

1 tablespoon dried oregano

1 tablespoon red wine vinegar

sea salt and freshly ground black pepper

SERVES 6

Salsa rossa is one of those divine Italian sauces that transforms simple meat and fish dishes into food nirvana. The slight sweetness from the peppers is a good foil for the spicy pepper crust.

To make the salsa rossa, grill the pepper until charred all over, then put into a plastic bag and let cool. Remove and discard the skin and seeds, reserving any juices, then chop the flesh.

Put the oil into a frying pan, heat gently, then add the garlic and sauté for 3 minutes. Add the tomatoes, chilli flakes and oregano and simmer gently for 15 minutes. Stir in the peppers and the vinegar and simmer for a further 5 minutes to evaporate any excess liquid.

Transfer to a blender and purée until fairly smooth. Add salt and pepper to taste and let cool. It may be stored in a screw-top jar in the refrigerator for up to 3 days.

Put the crushed peppercorns onto a large plate. Brush the tuna steaks with oil, then press the crushed peppercorns into the surface. Preheat a barbecue, add the tuna and cook for 1 minute on each side. Wrap loosely in foil and let rest for 5 minutes before serving with the salsa rossa and a salad of mixed leaves.

Dukkah is a Middle Eastern side dish comprising mixed nuts and spices, which are ground to a coarse powder and served as a dip for warm bread. Here, it is used as a coating for char-grilled tuna. Preserved lemons are available from good delicatessens, Middle Eastern food stores and some larger supermarkets.

dukkah crusted tuna
with preserved lemon salsa

4 tuna steaks, about 200 g each

3 tablespoons sesame seeds

2 tablespoons coriander seeds

½ tablespoon cumin seeds

25 g blanched almonds, chopped

½ teaspoon salt

freshly ground black pepper

olive oil, for brushing

Preserved lemon salsa

25 g preserved lemons

25 g semi-dried tomatoes

2 spring onions, very
finely chopped

1 tablespoon coarsely chopped
fresh parsley

3 tablespoons extra virgin olive oil

¼ teaspoon caster sugar

SERVES 4

To make the salsa, chop the preserved lemon and tomatoes finely and put into a bowl. Stir in the spring onions, parsley, olive oil and sugar and set aside until ready to serve.

Wash the tuna steaks under cold running water and pat dry with kitchen paper.

Put the sesame seeds into a dry frying pan and toast over medium heat until golden and aromatic. Remove and let cool. Repeat with the coriander seeds, cumin seeds and almonds. Transfer to a spice grinder (or clean coffee grinder) and grind roughly. Alternatively, use a mortar and pestle. Add the salt and a little pepper.

Preheat the barbecue. Brush the tuna steaks with olive oil and coat with the dukkah mixture. Cook over hot coals for 1 minute on each side, top with the salsa and serve.

900 g monkfish tail, cut into chunks

12–16 cherry tomatoes

1–2 teaspoons smoked paprika, to dust

1–2 lemons, cut into wedges, to serve

Chermoula

2 garlic cloves

1 teaspoon coarse sea salt

1–2 teaspoons cumin seeds, crushed or ground

1 fresh red chilli, deseeded and chopped

freshly squeezed juice of 1 lemon

2 tablespoons olive oil

a small bunch of fresh coriander, roughly chopped

4–6 metal skewers or 4–6 wooden skewers, soaked in water before use

SERVES 4–6

monkfish kebabs
with chermoula

Chermoula is a classic Moroccan flavouring of garlic, chilli, cumin and fresh coriander, which is employed as a marinade for fish and chicken tagines and grilled dishes. Any meaty, white fish can be used for this recipe but monkfish cooks particularly well over charcoal.

To make the chermoula, use a mortar and pestle to pound the garlic with the salt to a smooth paste. Add the cumin, chilli, lemon juice and olive oil and stir in the coriander.

Put the fish chunks in a shallow dish and rub with the chermoula. Cover and chill in the refrigerator for 1–2 hours.

Thread the marinated monkfish and cherry tomatoes alternately onto the skewers. Preheat the barbecue. Cook the kebabs for about 2 minutes on each side, until the monkfish is nicely browned. Dust with a little paprika and serve with wedges of lemon for squeezing over them.

about 30 preserved vine leaves

4–5 large, skinless fillets of white fish, with all bones removed

Marinade

2–3 garlic cloves, crushed

1–2 teaspoons ground cumin

4 tablespoons olive oil

freshly squeezed juice of 1 lemon

1 teaspoon sea salt

Tangy herb sauce

50 ml white wine vinegar or freshly squeezed lemon juice

1–2 tablespoons sugar

a pinch of saffron threads

1 onion, finely chopped

2 garlic cloves, finely chopped

2–3 spring onions, finely sliced

a thumb-sized piece of fresh ginger, peeled and grated

2 fresh hot red or green chillies, finely sliced

a small bunch of fresh coriander, finely chopped

a small bunch of fresh mint, finely chopped

sea salt

a packet of short wooden or bamboo skewers, soaked in water before use

SERVES 4

vine-wrapped fish kebabs
with tangy herb sauce

For these Mediterranean kebabs, almost any kind of firm, white fish fillet will do – monkfish or haddock work well. The fish is prepared in a simple marinade and then wrapped in the vine leaves, which become crisper with cooking whilst keeping the fish moist.

First wash the vine leaves and soak them in several changes of water for 1 hour.

To prepare the marinade, mix all the ingredients together in a shallow bowl. Cut each fillet of fish into roughly 8 bite-sized pieces and coat in the marinade. Cover and chill in the refrigerator for 1 hour.

Meanwhile, prepare the tangy herb sauce. Put the vinegar in a small saucepan with the sugar and 1–2 tablespoons water. Heat until the sugar has dissolved. Bring to the boil for 1 minute, then leave to cool. Add the other ingredients, mix well and spoon the sauce into small individual bowls.

Lay the prepared vine leaves on a flat surface and place a piece of marinated fish in the centre of each one. Fold the edges over the fish and wrap the leaf up into a small parcel. Push the parcels carefully onto the individual skewers and brush the leaves with any remaining marinade.

Preheat the barbecue. Cook the kebabs for 2–3 minutes on each side. Serve immediately with a dish of tangy herb sauce on the side for dipping.

This is a great way to cook clams on the barbecue, where all the wonderful juices are collected in the foil parcel. Mop them up with plenty of crusty bread.

clam parcels
with garlic butter

1 kg vongole clams

125 g unsalted butter, softened

grated zest and freshly squeezed juice of ½ unwaxed lemon

2 garlic cloves, crushed

2 tablespoons chopped fresh parsley

freshly ground black pepper

fresh crusty bread, to serve

SERVES 4

Wash the clams under cold running water and scrub the shells. Discard any with broken shells or any that refuse to close when tapped lightly with a knife. Shake the clams dry and divide between 4 pieces of foil.

Put the butter, lemon zest and juice, garlic, parsley and pepper into a bowl and beat well, then divide equally between the clams. Wrap the foil over the clams and seal the edges to form parcels.

Preheat the barbecue, then put the parcels onto the grill rack and cook for 5 minutes. Check 1 parcel to see if the clams have opened and serve if ready or cook a little longer, if needed. Serve with crusty bread.

500 g fresh, large prawns, deveined and trimmed of heads, feelers and legs

leaves from a small bunch of fresh coriander, to serve

2–4 fresh green chillies, deseeded and sliced, to serve

Marinade

3 tablespoons tamarind pulp*

2 tablespoons sweet soy sauce

1 tablespoon sugar

freshly ground black pepper

a packet of wooden or bamboo skewers, soaked in water before use

SERVES 2–4

char-grilled tamarind prawns

This is popular street food in Malaysia and Indonesia. The aroma emanating from the stalls as the marinated prawns are grilled over charcoal, makes you feel very hungry.

Rinse the prepared prawns well, pat dry and using a very sharp knife, make an incision along the curve of the tail. Set aside.

Put the tamarind pulp in a bowl and add 250 ml of warm water. Soak the pulp, until soft, squeezing it with your fingers to help dissolve it. Strain the liquid and discard any fibre or seeds. In a bowl, mix together the tamarind juice, soy sauce, sugar and black pepper. Pour it over the prawns, rubbing it over the shells and into the incision in the tails. Cover, refrigerate and leave to marinate for about 1 hour.

Preheat the barbecue. Insert a skewer into each marinated prawn. Cook the prawns for about 3 minutes on each side, until the prawn shells have turned orange, brushing them with the marinade as they cook. Serve immediately, garnished with the coriander leaves and chillies.

*Note Tamarind lends a rich, sweet-sour flavour to dishes. The tropical trees produce fresh pods that are either sold fresh or processed into pulp or paste for convenience and long shelf life. You may think you've never tried tamarind, however it is an essential ingredient in several traditional British condiments, most notably brown sauce. Look out for it in Caribbean markets – semi-dried tamarind pulp comes in soft rectangular blocks wrapped in plastic. The darker concentrated paste is sold in tubs and is a more processed product.

prawns with chilli oil and pistachio and mint pesto

Prawns make the fastest, freshest, most impressive dish you can imagine. If you can't find uncooked prawns, use precooked ones – just sprinkle them with the chilli oil and lemon juice and serve with the cool and refreshing pesto.

24 large uncooked prawns, shelled and deveined

4 tablespoons chilli oil*

freshly squeezed juice of 1 lemon

fresh crusty bread, to serve

Pistachio and mint pesto

50 g shelled pistachio nuts

a bunch of fresh mint

1 garlic clove, crushed

2 spring onions, chopped

125 ml extra virgin olive oil

1 tablespoon white wine vinegar

sea salt and freshly ground black pepper

a packet of wooden or bamboo skewers, soaked in water before use

SERVES 4

To make the pesto, put the nuts, mint, garlic and spring onions into a food processor and grind coarsely. Add the oil and purée until fairly smooth and green. Stir in the vinegar and season to taste. Set aside while you prepare the prawns, or store in the refrigerator for up to 5 days.

Put the prawns into a shallow dish and sprinkle with the chilli oil, salt and pepper. Cover and let marinate for at least 30 minutes or longer, if possible.

When ready to serve, thread the prawns onto skewers and cook on a preheated barbecue for about 2 minutes on each side until charred and tender – the flesh should be just opaque. Do not overcook or the prawns will be tough.

Serve on separate plates or a large platter, sprinkle with fresh lemon juice and serve with the pesto and crusty bread to mop up the juices.

*Note Olive oils infused with chilli and other flavourings are widely available in most supermarkets or gourmet food stores.

char-grilled prawns
with avocado chilli salsa

3–5 uncooked prawns per person, depending on size, with shells

2 tablespoons chilli oil

freshly squeezed juice of 2 limes

a pinch of sea salt

2 tablespoons brown sugar

Avocado chilli salsa

2 red onions, quartered, then finely sliced

1 red chilli, deseeded and sliced or diced

finely grated zest and freshly squeezed juice of 1 unwaxed lime

2 large, ripe Hass avocados, halved, with stones removed*

2 ripe red tomatoes, halved, deseeded and diced

a large handful of fresh coriander

sea salt and coarsely cracked black pepper

SERVES 4

Avocado is a Mexican ingredient, so it tastes good in a salsa (which is, after all, a Latin American dish). For this recipe, use the warty-skinned, greenish-purple Hass avocado, which are the most flavoursome.

To make the salsa, put the onion, chilli and half the lime juice into a bowl and set aside to marinate for a few minutes.

Using a small teaspoon or coffee spoon, scoop out small balls of avocado into a serving bowl. Add the lime zest and remaining juice and turn gently to coat.

Add the diced tomatoes to the onion mixture, toss gently, then add the avocado. Tear the coriander leaves over the top and sprinkle with the sea salt and black pepper.

Meanwhile, slit the prawns down the back and pull out the black vein, if any. Put the chilli oil, lime juice, salt and sugar into a bowl, add the prawns and toss to coat. Using your fingers, push the sauce into the slit and set aside for 30 minutes. Preheat a barbecue to medium hot, add the prawns, then cook on both sides until just opaque.

Serve the prawns with the avocado chilli salsa. Flour tortillas, warmed on the barbecue, soured cream and lettuce are also delicious accompaniments.

*Note Always prepare avocado at the last moment and coat in a little citrus juice. Avocado turns brown very quickly – don't believe the old wives' tale that the stone prevents this.

12 large fresh prawns, shelled
to the tail

8 fresh scallops, shelled and
thoroughly cleaned

8 cherry tomatoes

1 green pepper, cut into
bite-sized squares

Marinade

freshly squeezed juice of 2 lemons

4 garlic cloves, crushed

1 teaspoon ground cumin

1 teaspoon paprika

sea salt

Walnut sauce

115 g shelled walnut halves

2 slices day-old bread, soaked
in water and squeezed dry

2–3 garlic cloves, crushed

3–4 tablespoons olive oil

freshly squeezed juice of 1 lemon

a dash of white wine vinegar

sea salt and freshly ground
black pepper

*a packet of wooden or bamboo
skewers, soaked in water
before use*

SERVES 4

prawn and scallop kebabs
with walnut sauce

**This is one of the most popular ways to enjoy the jumbo
prawns and scallops along the Mediterranean coast of
Syria, Turkey and Lebanon. Threaded onto skewers with
peppers and tomatoes, they are served char-grilled with
a delicious garlicky walnut sauce.**

To make the marinade, mix together the lemon juice, garlic,
cumin, paprika and a little salt in a bowl. Rub the mixture into the
prawns and scallops. Cover, refrigerate and leave to marinate for
about 1 hour.

Meanwhile, prepare the walnut sauce. Using a mortar and
pestle, pound the walnuts to a paste, or whizz them in a food
processor. Add the bread and garlic and pound to a paste.
Drizzle in the olive oil, stirring all the time, and beat in the lemon
juice and vinegar. The sauce should be smooth with the
consistency of thick double cream – if it's too dry, stir in a little
water. Season the sauce with salt and pepper and set aside.

Thread the prawns and scallops onto the skewers, alternating
with the tomatoes and green pepper, until all the ingredients
are used up. Preheat the barbecue. Cook the kebabs for 2
minutes on each side, basting with any of the leftover marinade,
until the prawn shells are orange, the scallops tender and the
tomatoes and peppers lightly browned. Serve hot with the walnut
sauce on the side for dipping.

skewered scallops
with coconut dressing

Seafood has a natural affinity with coconut, and it is a combination often found in Indonesian and Thai cooking. The tangy lime and chilli marinade cuts wonderfully through the richness of the sweet coconut and succulent, meaty scallops.

24 large king scallops, without corals

2 tablespoons peanut oil

grated zest of 2 limes

2 red chillies, deseeded and chopped

2 teaspoons grated fresh ginger

1 garlic clove, crushed

1 tablespoon Thai fish sauce

Coconut milk dressing

125 ml coconut milk

1 tablespoon Thai fish sauce

2 teaspoons caster sugar

2 teaspoons coconut or rice wine vinegar*

6 wooden or bamboo skewers, soaked in water before use

SERVES 6

Trim the tough white muscle from the side of each scallop. Put the scallops into a shallow non-metal dish.

Put the peanut oil, lime zest, chillies, ginger, garlic and fish sauce into a small jug or bowl, mix well, then pour over the scallops. Let marinate in the refrigerator for 1 hour.

To make the dressing, put the coconut milk, fish sauce, sugar and vinegar into a small saucepan, heat gently to dissolve the sugar, then bring to a gentle simmer until thickened slightly. Remove from the heat and let cool completely.

Meanwhile, preheat the barbecue until hot.

Thread the scallops onto the prepared skewers and cook for 1 minute on each side. Don't overcook or the scallops will be tough. Serve with the coconut dressing and wedges of lime.

*Note Coconut or palm vinegar are used in Thailand and the Philippines: both are milder than regular vinegars. Buy them in Asian food stores or use white rice vinegar as an alternative.

Piri-piri, a Portuguese chilli condiment traditionally used to baste grilled chicken, is a combination of chopped red chillies, olive oil and vinegar. It is generally very hot and only a drizzle is needed to add spice to grilled food. In this recipe the heat is tempered, but you can use more chillies if you like it hotter. It works very well with squid.

squid piri-piri

8 medium squid tubes, about 250 g each*

freshly squeezed juice of 1 lemon, plus extra lemon wedges, to serve

sea salt

Piri-piri sauce

8 small red chillies

300 ml extra virgin olive oil

1 tablespoon white wine vinegar

sea salt and freshly ground black pepper

16 wooden or bamboo skewers, soaked in water before use

SERVES 4

To prepare the squid, put the squid tube on a board and, using a sharp knife, cut down one side and open the tube out flat. Scrape away any remaining insides and wash and dry well.

Skewer each opened-out tube with 2 skewers, running them up the long sides of each piece. Rub a little sea salt over each one and squeeze over the lemon juice. Marinate in the refrigerator for 30 minutes.

Meanwhile, to make the piri-piri, finely chop the whole chillies without deseeding them and transfer to a small jar or bottle. Add the oil, vinegar and a little salt and pepper. Shake well and set aside.

Meanwhile, preheat a barbecue until hot.

Baste the squid with a little of the piri-piri and cook for 1–1½ minutes on each side until charred. Drizzle with extra sauce and serve with lemon wedges.

*Note If the squid includes the tentacles, cut them off in one piece, thread with a skewer and cook and marinate in the same way as the tubes.

vegetables

2 aubergines, cut into chunks

2 courgettes, cut into chunks

2–3 peppers, stalks removed, deseeded and cut into chunks

12–16 cherry tomatoes

4 red onions, cut into quarters

Marinade

4 tablespoons olive oil

freshly squeezed juice of ½ a lemon

2 garlic cloves, crushed

1 teaspoon sea salt

Garlicky pesto

3–4 garlic cloves, roughly chopped

leaves from a large bunch of fresh basil (at least 30–40 leaves)

½ teaspoon sea salt

2–3 tablespoons pine nuts

extra virgin olive oil, as required

about 60 g freshly grated Parmesan cheese

4–6 metal skewers or wooden skewers, soaked in water before use

SERVES 4–6

summer vegetable kebabs
with homemade garlicky pesto

Full of sunshine flavours, these kebabs can be served with couscous and a salad, or with pasta tossed in some of the pesto sauce. Homemade pesto is very personal – some people like it very garlicky, as in this recipe, others prefer lots of basil or Parmesan – so simply adjust the quantities to suit your taste.

To make the pesto, use a mortar and pestle to pound the garlic with the basil leaves and salt – the salt will act as an abrasive and help to grind. (If you only have a small mortar and pestle, you may have to do this in batches.) Add the pine nuts and pound them to a paste. Slowly drizzle in some olive oil and bind with the grated Parmesan. Continue to pound and grind with the pestle, adding in enough oil to make a smooth sauce. Set aside.

Put all the prepared vegetables in a bowl. Mix together the olive oil, lemon juice, garlic and salt and pour it over the vegetables. Using your hands, toss the vegetables gently in the marinade, then thread them onto the skewers.

Preheat the barbecue. Cook the kebabs for 2–3 minutes on each side, until the vegetables are nicely browned. Serve the kebabs with the pesto on the side for drizzling.

Mushrooms, with their meaty texture and earthy flavour, provide vegetarians with a great meat-free alternative to hamburgers. Here they are served with a garlic sauce, but you can also serve them traditionally with mustard, salad, cheese and pickles.

mushroom burgers
with caramelized garlic aïoli

8 large portobello mushrooms

4–6 tablespoons olive oil

4 large burger buns, halved

4 tablespoons Chilli Relish (page 53)

a handful of rocket

sea salt and freshly ground black pepper

Caramelized garlic aïoli

1 large head garlic

2 egg yolks

1 teaspoon Dijon mustard

1 teaspoon freshly squeezed lemon juice

200 ml olive oil

SERVES 4

To make the aïoli, wrap the garlic head in foil and bake in a preheated oven at 200°C (400°F) Gas 6 for 45–50 minutes until the garlic is really soft. Let cool, then squeeze the garlic purée out of each clove into a bowl.

Put the egg yolks, mustard, lemon juice, salt and the garlic purée in a food processor and blend briefly until frothy. With the blade running, gradually pour in the oil through the funnel until the sauce is thickened and all the oil incorporated. Transfer the aïoli to a bowl, cover the surface with clingfilm and chill until required.

Peel the mushroom caps and trim the stalks so they are flat with the cups. Brush lightly with olive oil, season with salt and pepper and barbecue or grill for 4–5 minutes on each side until softened and cooked through.

Toast the buns and fill with the mushrooms, caramelized garlic aïoli, chilli relish and some rocket. Serve hot.

32 large fresh bay leaves

20 small beetroot

20 baby onions, unpeeled

3 tablespoons extra virgin olive oil

1 tablespoon balsamic vinegar

sea salt and freshly ground black pepper

8 metal skewers

SERVES 4

For this dish, you need beetroot and baby onions of roughly the same size, so they will cook evenly on the barbecue. Vegetable brochettes are an excellent accompaniment to grilled meats or fish, or a good vegetarian alternative.

beetroot and baby onion brochettes

Put the bay leaves into a bowl, cover with cold water and let soak for 1 hour before cooking.

Cut the stalks off the beetroot and wash well under cold running water. Put the beetroot and baby onions into a large saucepan of lightly salted boiling water and blanch for 5 minutes. Drain and refresh under cold running water. Pat dry with kitchen paper, then peel the onions.

Preheat the barbecue. Thread the beetroot, onions and damp bay leaves onto the skewers, sprinkle with the olive oil and vinegar and season well with salt and pepper. Cook over medium hot coals for 20–25 minutes, turning occasionally, until charred and tender, then serve.

225 g dried chickpeas

1 small onion, finely chopped

2 garlic cloves, crushed

½ bunch of fresh flat leaf parsley

½ bunch of fresh coriander

2 teaspoons ground coriander

½ teaspoon baking powder

4 soft oval rolls

a handful of salad leaves

2 tomatoes, diced

sea salt and freshly
ground black pepper

sunflower or peanut oil,
for shallow frying

Tahini yoghurt sauce

125 g Greek or thick yoghurt

1 tablespoon tahini paste

1 garlic clove, crushed

½ tablespoon freshly squeezed
lemon juice

1 tablespoon extra virgin olive oil

SERVES 4

spiced falafel burger

Falafels are Egyptian bean patties traditionally served in pita bread with salad leaves and hoummus. Here they make a great burger filling with a tangy yoghurt dressing. These burgers do need to be fried to prevent them becoming dry, but they can be finished for a minute or two on the barbecue to give them a slight smoky flavour before serving.

Put the dried chickpeas in a bowl and add cold water to cover by a good 12 cm. Let soak overnight. Drain the chickpeas well, transfer to a food processor and blend until coarsely ground. Add the onion, garlic, parsley, fresh and ground coriander, baking powder and some salt and pepper and blend until very smooth. Transfer to a bowl, cover and chill for 30 minutes.

To make the tahini sauce, put the yoghurt, tahini, garlic, lemon juice and olive oil in a bowl and whisk until smooth. Season to taste with salt and pepper and set aside until required.

Using wet hands, shape the chickpea mixture into 12 small or 8 medium patties. Heat a shallow layer of sunflower oil in a frying pan, add the patties and fry for 3 minutes on each side until golden and cooked through. Drain on kitchen paper.

Cut the rolls in half and fill with 2–3 patties, tahini yoghurt sauce, salad leaves and diced tomato. Serve hot.

grilled corn
with chilli salt rub

6 corn cobs, husks removed

2 tablespoons extra virgin olive oil, plus extra to serve

3 ancho chillies

1½ tablespoons sea salt

3 limes, cut into wedges

SERVES 6

One of America's most popular chillies is the ancho, the dried version of the poblano. When ground to a fine powder, it has a smoky flavour and is mild to medium on the heat scale – delicious with the sweet, nutty taste of corn.

Trim the ends of the corn. Bring a large saucepan of lightly salted water to the boil, add the corn and boil for 5 minutes. Drain and refresh under cold water. Pat dry.

Preheat a barbecue or grill until hot. Brush the corn with oil and cook on the barbecue or under the grill for 6–8 minutes, turning frequently until charred all over.

Meanwhile, remove the stalk and seeds from the dried chillies. Chop the flesh coarsely and, using a spice grinder or mortar and pestle, grind to a fine powder. Transfer to a small bowl, then mix in the salt.

Rub the lime wedges vigorously over the corn, sprinkle with the chilli salt and serve with extra oil for drizzling.

chunky aubergine burgers with pesto

1 large aubergine, about 750 g

4 tablespoons extra virgin olive oil

1 tablespoon balsamic vinegar

1 garlic clove, crushed

4 soft bread rolls, halved

2 beefsteak tomatoes,
thickly sliced

200 g mozzarella cheese, sliced

a handful of rocket

sea salt and freshly ground
black pepper

Pesto

50 g fresh basil leaves

1 garlic clove, crushed

4 tablespoons pine nuts

7 tablespoons extra virgin olive oil

2 tablespoons freshly grated
Parmesan cheese

SERVES 4

The smoky taste of char-grilled aubergines and the basil pesto give these burgers a distinctive Mediterranean flavour. You could replace the fresh beefsteak tomatoes with semi-dried tomatoes if you like.

To make the pesto, put the basil, garlic, pine nuts, oil and some salt and pepper in a food processor and blend until fairly smooth. Transfer to a bowl, stir in the Parmesan and add more salt and pepper to taste. Set aside until required.

Cut the aubergine into 1 cm slices. Put the oil, vinegar, garlic, salt and pepper in a bowl, whisk to mix, then brush over the aubergine slices. Grill them on a preheated hot barbecue for 3–4 minutes on each side until charred and softened.

Lightly toast the rolls and top with a slice of aubergine. Spread with pesto, add another slice of aubergine, then add a slice of tomato and mozzarella. Drizzle with more pesto, then top with a few rocket leaves. Put the tops on the rolls and serve hot.

4 medium roasting potatoes,
such as King Edward or Desirée

butter

sea salt and freshly ground
black pepper

SERVES 4

ember-roasted potatoes

**Roasting potatoes on the barbecue is so easy and the
result is a beautiful crispy skin and soft, fluffy insides.
Just wrap them in foil and leave them to sit in the embers
while you cook your meat and fish on the grill above.**

Wrap the potatoes individually in a double layer of foil and,
as soon as the coals are glowing red, put the potatoes on top.
Rake the charcoal up and around them, but without covering
them. Let cook for about 25 minutes, then, using tongs, turn
the potatoes over carefully and cook for a further 25–30 minutes
until cooked through.

Remove from the heat and carefully remove the foil, then cut
the potatoes in half. Serve, topped with a spoonful of butter,
salt and pepper.

Variation

To cook sweet potatoes, follow the same method but cook for
about 20 minutes on each side.

Sweet potatoes are perfect for the barbecue because they cook quickly without pre-boiling. When tossed in dressing and wrapped in foil, the potatoes steam cook and absorb the flavours of the dressing. Care must be taken so that the potatoes do not burn through the foil where they are in direct contact with the heat. This recipe calls for individual packets, but one large packet does just as well. Cook them before the meat and put them on one side of the barbecue to keep warm.

4 large sweet potatoes, about 600 g, peeled and cut into 4 or 5 slices

1–2 tablespoons vegetable oil

1–2 tablespoons shoyu or tamari soy sauce

1 tablespoon sesame seeds

1 tablespoon finely chopped fresh parsley, to serve

a barbecue with a lid

SERVES 4

sesame sweet potato packets

Put the sweet potato in a bowl with the oil, soy sauce and sesame seeds and toss well. Divide between 4 large squares of aluminium foil, then crinkle the foil up around them and close tightly. Put the foil packets on a preheated hot barbecue, close the lid and leave to cook for 20–30 minutes or until tender. Alternatively, place the foil packets on a baking tray and bake in a preheated oven at 180°C (350°F) Gas 4 for 20 minutes or until tender.

When ready to serve, open up the packets and sprinkle a little parsley on the sweet potatoes.

Note An even easier way to cook sesame sweet potatoes is to boil the potatoes for 4–5 minutes or until tender, then drain and put in a bowl. Add the soy sauce, sesame seeds and parsley and toss well.

Truly at home in both Middle Eastern and Mediterranean cuisines, aubergines are compatible with endless spices, herbs and a multitude of other ingredients. In this dish, they soak up the fragrance of the spices and are perfectly paired with smoked cheese, enhancing the already smoky barbecue flavour.

aubergine and smoked cheese rolls

2 aubergines, cut lengthways into about 5 slices

1 teaspoon chilli oil

125 ml olive oil

3 teaspoons cumin seeds, lightly toasted in a dry frying pan and ground

2 garlic cloves, crushed

1 red chilli, deseeded and finely chopped

a large handful of fresh mint leaves, finely chopped

175 g firm smoked cheese, sliced

sea salt and freshly ground black pepper

a large handful of fresh coriander, coarsely chopped, to serve

freshly squeezed juice of ½ lemon, to serve

MAKES 10 ROLLS

Arrange the aubergine slices on a large tray. Mix the chilli and olive oils, cumin, garlic, chilli, mint, salt and pepper in a measuring jug, then pour over the aubergines. Turn each slice over so that both sides are well coated. Cover with clingfilm and set aside for a few hours or overnight to soak up all the flavours.

Put the aubergine on a preheated barbecue or smoking-hot stove-top grill pan. Cook for about 4 minutes, then turn and cook the other side until tender and browned.

Remove from the heat, put some of the cheese at one end of a slice of aubergine and roll up firmly (do this while the aubergine is still hot so the cheese melts). Repeat with the other slices. Sprinkle with the coriander and lemon juice, then serve.

300 g tofu, rinsed, drained, patted dry and cut into bite-sized cubes

leaves from a small bunch of fresh basil, shredded

sesame oil, for frying

Marinade

3 lemongrass stalks, trimmed and finely chopped

1 tablespoon peanut oil

3 tablespoons soy sauce

1–2 fresh red chillies, deseeded and finely chopped

2 garlic cloves, crushed

1 teaspoon ground turmeric

2 teaspoons sugar

sea salt

Soy dipping sauce

4–5 tablespoons soy sauce

1–2 tablespoons Thai fish sauce

freshly squeezed juice of 1 lime

1–2 teaspoons sugar

1 fresh red chilli, deseeded and finely chopped

a packet of wooden or bamboo skewers, soaked in water before use

SERVES 3–4

spicy tofu satay
with soy dipping sauce

Here is a very tasty dish that does wonderful things to tofu, which can be rather bland. Full of the flavours of Southeast Asia, this tasty Vietnamese snack is perfect as part of a vegetarian selection at a barbecue party, but is sure to be enjoyed by all!

To make the marinade, mix the lemongrass, peanut oil, soy sauce, chilli, garlic and turmeric with the sugar until it has dissolved. Add a little salt to taste and toss in the tofu, making sure it is well coated. Leave to marinate for 1 hour.

Prepare the soy dipping sauce by whisking all the ingredients together. Set aside until ready to serve.

Preheat the barbecue. Thread the tofu cubes onto the skewers and grill them for 2–3 minutes on each side. Serve the tofu hot, garnished with the shredded basil and with the dipping sauce on the side.

plantain with lime and chilli

2 plantains, thinly sliced diagonally

freshly squeezed juice of 1 lime

1 tablespoon chilli oil

sea salt

fresh coriander, coarsely chopped, to serve

SERVES 4

Plantain lends itself very well to barbecues and grill pans. The cooking process brings out its sweetness, so it's good to offset that with a bit of citrus and chilli. Plantain is readily available from some supermarkets or speciality Caribbean shops.

Put the slices of plantain in a large bowl with the lime juice and chilli oil. Carefully turn them over to cover evenly (this will stop them discolouring).

Arrange the slices on a preheated barbecue or stove-top grill pan and cook for 2–3 minutes or until slightly charred. Gently turn them over, using a palette knife, then cook the other side for 2 minutes. (The plantain changes from a fleshy colour to a beautiful bright yellow blackened with the stripes of the pan or barbecue.)

When cooked, lift onto a plate, sprinkle with salt and fresh coriander, then serve.

Note When plantains are ripe and at their best for cooking, they have blackened skins and look like ordinary bananas that have gone past their best.

salads & sides

mayonnaise

Mayonnaise is the perfect accompaniment to barbecued foods, and homemade is all the better. When making it, try to use a regular olive oil rather than extra virgin, which can make the sauce bitter.

2 egg yolks

2 teaspoons white wine vinegar or lemon juice

2 teaspoons Dijon mustard

¼ teaspoon salt

300 ml olive oil

freshly ground black pepper

MAKES ABOUT 300 ML

Put the egg yolks, vinegar, mustard and salt into a food processor and blend briefly until frothy. With the machine running, gradually pour in the olive oil in a slow steady stream until all the oil is incorporated and the sauce is thick and glossy.

If the sauce is too thick, add 1–2 tablespoons boiling water and blend again briefly. Season to taste with salt and pepper, then cover the surface of the mayonnaise with clingfilm. Store in the refrigerator for up to 3 days.

creamy coleslaw

No barbecue would be complete without a classic coleslaw on the side. This one uses homemade mayonnaise, but if you are short on time you can always substitute with a shop-bought brand.

250 g white cabbage, thinly sliced

175 g carrots, grated

½ white onion, thinly sliced

1 teaspoon salt

2 teaspoons caster sugar

1 tablespoon white wine vinegar

50 g Mayonnaise (left)

2 tablespoons double cream

1 tablespoon wholegrain mustard

sea salt and freshly ground black pepper

SERVES 4

Put the white cabbage, carrots and onion into a colander and sprinkle with the salt, sugar and vinegar. Stir well and let drain over a bowl for 30 minutes.

Squeeze out excess liquid from the vegetables and put into a large bowl. Put the mayonnaise, cream and mustard into a separate bowl and mix well, then stir into the cabbage mixture. Season to taste with salt and pepper and serve. Store in the refrigerator for up to 3 days.

This satisfying summer salad with a delicious hint of fresh mint makes a superb accompaniment to barbecued meat or fish. It also makes a great vegetarian option.

courgette, feta and mint salad

1 tablespoon sesame seeds

6 large courgettes

3 tablespoons extra virgin olive oil

150 g feta cheese, crumbled

a handful of fresh mint leaves

Dressing

4 tablespoons extra virgin olive oil

1 tablespoon lemon juice

1 small garlic clove, crushed

sea salt and freshly ground black pepper

SERVES 4

Put the sesame seeds into a dry frying pan and toast over medium heat until golden and aromatic. Remove from the heat, let cool and set aside until required.

Preheat the barbecue. Cut the courgettes diagonally into thick slices, toss with the olive oil and season with salt and pepper. Cook over hot coals for 2–3 minutes on each side until charred and tender. Remove and let cool.

Put all the dressing ingredients into a screw-top jar and shake well. Add salt and pepper to taste.

Put the courgettes, feta and mint into a large bowl, add the dressing and toss well until evenly coated. Sprinkle with the sesame seeds and serve at once.

Vegetables taste wonderful when cooked on the barbecue – it brings out their natural sweetness. Look out for the long, thin red peppers (ramiro or romano) when available – they are particularly good grilled. This salad serves four as a main course or six as a starter.

salad of roasted peppers and asparagus

½ red onion, sliced

6 sweet red peppers

500 g asparagus spears, trimmed

extra virgin olive oil, for brushing

250 g mangetout

75 g mixed salad leaves

a handful of fresh parsley and dill leaves

50 g hazelnuts, toasted and coarsely chopped

Hazelnut oil dressing

4 tablespoons hazelnut oil

2 tablespoons extra virgin olive oil

1 tablespoon sherry vinegar

1 teaspoon caster sugar

sea salt and freshly ground black pepper

SERVES 4–6

Put the sliced onion into a sieve, sprinkle with salt and let drain over a bowl for 30 minutes. Rinse under cold running water and pat dry with kitchen paper.

Preheat the barbecue, then cook the peppers over hot coals for 15 minutes, turning frequently until charred all over. Transfer to a plastic bag, seal and let soften until cool. Peel off the skin and discard the seeds, then cut the flesh into thick strips.

Brush the asparagus with olive oil and cook over hot coals for 3–4 minutes, turning frequently, until charred and tender.

Put the mangetout into a large saucepan of lightly salted boiling water and boil for 1–2 minutes. Drain and refresh under cold running water.

Put the onion, peppers, asparagus and mangetout into a large bowl and toss gently. Add the salad leaves, herbs and hazelnuts. Put the dressing ingredients into a bowl and whisk well, then pour over the salad and toss until coated. Serve.

250 g fresh mozzarella cheese, drained

1 large green pepper, deseeded and chopped

1 Lebanese (mini) cucumber, chopped

2 ripe tomatoes, chopped

½ red onion, finely chopped

2 pita breads

4 tablespoons extra virgin olive oil

freshly squeezed juice of ½ lemon

sea salt and freshly ground black pepper

Olive salsa

75 g Kalamata olives, pitted and chopped

1 tablespoon chopped fresh parsley

1 small garlic clove, finely chopped

4 tablespoons extra virgin olive oil

1 tablespoon freshly squeezed lemon juice

freshly ground black pepper

SERVES 4

grilled pita salad
with olive salsa and mozzarella

Fatoush is a bread salad made from grilled pita bread. It's often accompanied by haloumi, a firm cheese that can be char-grilled. This recipe uses fresh mozzarella cheese, which can also be cooked on the grill and picks up an appealing smokiness in the process.

Wrap the mozzarella in kitchen paper and squeeze gently to remove excess water. Unwrap and cut into thick slices. Brush the slices well with olive oil and place them on the barbecue grill. Cook over the hot coals for 1 minute on each side until the cheese is charred with lines and beginning to soften. Alternatively, simply slice the cheese and use without grilling.

Put the green pepper, cucumber, tomatoes and onion into a bowl. Toast the pita breads over hot coals, cool slightly, then tear into bite-sized pieces. Add to the bowl, then pour over the olive oil and lemon juice. Season and stir well.

Put all the ingredients for the olive salsa into a bowl and stir well.

Spoon the salad onto small plates, top with a few slices of mozzarella and some olive salsa, then serve.

tabbouleh with chickpeas and spring salad

90 g fine bulghur (cracked wheat)

2 tablespoons freshly squeezed lemon juice

60 ml extra virgin olive oil

1 small punnet of cherry tomatoes, halved

1 large handful of fresh mint leaves, finely chopped

2 tablespoons finely chopped dill

1 small bunch of fresh flat leaf parsley, finely chopped

400 g canned chickpeas, rinsed and drained

120–150 g spring salad mix

sea salt and freshly ground black pepper

toasted Turkish flat bread, to serve

SERVES 4

It's fun to hand-pick salad leaves, making up your own mix. You will find big barrels or bags of lovely tender spring salad leaves at your local market. When buying leaves, keep in mind you will need about two large handfuls per person. Avoid limp looking greens. If they do wilt a little on the way home on warmer days, give them a quick bath in a bowl of cold water with a pinch or two of sugar thrown in. This will freshen them up. The spring fresh ingredients are combined here with bulghur. Simply cover with boiling water to soften and add to your favourite salad ingredients.

Put the bulghur in a heatproof bowl and pour over 125 ml boiling water. Stir once, cover tightly with clingfilm and set aside for 8–10 minutes. Put the lemon juice and olive oil in a small bowl and whisk. Pour over the bulghur and stir well with a fork, fluffing up the bulghur and separating the grains.

Put the bulghur in a large bowl with the tomatoes, mint, dill, parsley, chickpeas and salad leaves. Use your hands to toss everything together. Season well with salt and pepper. Transfer to a serving plate and serve with toasted Turkish flat bread.

Tabbouleh, the fresh parsley salad from Lebanon, is based on bulghur wheat. This one is made with couscous, the fine Moroccan pasta, available in an instant version – you just soak it in water or stock for 10 minutes or so. It makes a quick and easy side for a barbecue and the grains soak up the lovely meat or fish juices and add flavour.

300 g instant couscous

freshly squeezed juice of 1 lemon

2 tablespoons chopped fresh basil

2 tablespoons chopped fresh coriander

2 tablespoons chopped fresh mint

2 tablespoons chopped fresh parsley

sea salt and freshly ground black pepper

2 lemons, halved, to serve

Fragrant garlic oil

1 whole head of garlic, cloves separated

2 bay leaves

600 ml extra virgin olive oil

SERVES 4

fragrant herb couscous salad

To make the fragrant garlic oil, peel the cloves and put them into a saucepan. Add the bay leaves and oil and heat gently for 15 minutes until the garlic has softened. Don't let the garlic brown. Let cool, remove and mash the garlic cloves, then return them to the oil. Refrigerate until required. Use 150 ml for this recipe and reserve the remainder.

Put the couscous into a bowl, add boiling water to cover by 5 cm and let soak for 10 minutes.

Drain the soaked couscous, shaking the sieve well to remove any excess water. Transfer to a bowl, add the fragrant garlic oil, lemon juice, chopped basil, coriander, mint and parsley. Season with salt and pepper, then set aside to develop the flavours until ready to serve. Serve with halved lemons.

2 teaspoons sea salt

175 g instant polenta

2 garlic cloves, crushed

1 tablespoon chopped fresh basil

50 g butter

50 g freshly grated
Parmesan cheese

freshly ground black pepper

olive oil, for brushing

*a rectangular cake tin,
23 x 30 cm, greased*

SERVES 8

grilled polenta

Grilled polenta triangles make a lovely accompaniment for grilled meats and fish or they can be used as a bruschetta-type base for grilled vegetables.

Pour 1 litre water into a heavy-based saucepan and bring to the boil. Add the salt and gradually whisk in the polenta in a steady stream, using a large, metal whisk.

Cook over low heat, stirring constantly with a wooden spoon for 5 minutes or until the grains have swelled and thickened.

Remove the saucepan from the heat and immediately beat in the garlic, basil, butter and Parmesan until the mixture is smooth. Season to taste with black pepper. Pour into the greased tin and let cool completely.

Preheat the barbecue. Turn out the polenta onto a board and cut into large squares, then cut in half again to form triangles. Brush the triangles with a little olive oil and cook over hot coals for 2–3 minutes on each side until charred and heated through.

chilli cornbread

75 g plain flour

1 tablespoon baking powder

200 g medium cornmeal or polenta

1 teaspoon salt

3 eggs, beaten

300 ml buttermilk

4 tablespoons extra virgin olive oil

200 g canned sweetcorn kernels, drained

1–2 red chillies, deseeded and chopped

2 tablespoons chopped fresh coriander

a deep loaf tin, 1 kg, greased and base-lined

SERVES 8–12

This flavoursome cornbread is great served in chunks to mop up the delicious juices of barbecued meat, fish or vegetables. It is handy to cook it in a deep loaf tin so that later it can be sliced and toasted more easily. However, if you are short of time, pour the mixture into a greased and base-lined baking tin and cook for 20–25 minutes.

Preheat the oven to 200°C (400°F) Gas 6.

Sift the flour and baking powder into a bowl and stir in the cornmeal and salt.

Mix the eggs, buttermilk and oil in a second bowl, then, using a wooden spoon, stir into the dry ingredients to make a smooth batter. Stir in the corn, chilli and coriander and pour into the prepared loaf tin.

Bake in the preheated oven for 40 minutes. Let cool in the tin for 5 minutes, then remove from the tin and let cool on a wire rack.

grilled rosemary flatbread

250 g strong white flour, plus extra for dusting

1½ teaspoons fast-acting yeast

1 teaspoon salt

1 tablespoon chopped fresh rosemary

2 tablespoons extra virgin olive oil, plus extra for brushing

SERVES 4

Hot from the grill, this aromatic herb bread is delicious used to mop up any wonderful meat juices, or eaten on its own with olive oil for dipping.

Sift the flour into the bowl of an electric mixer and stir in the yeast, salt and rosemary. Add 120 ml of hot water and the olive oil and knead with the dough hook at high speed for about 8 minutes or until the dough is smooth and elastic.

Alternatively, sift the flour into a large bowl and stir in the yeast, salt and rosemary. Make a well in the centre, then add the hot water and olive oil and mix to form a soft dough. Turn out onto a lightly floured work surface and knead until the dough is smooth and elastic.

Shape the dough into a ball, then put into an oiled bowl, cover with a tea towel and let rise in a warm place for 45–60 minutes or until doubled in size.

Punch down the dough and divide into quarters. Roll each piece out on a lightly floured work surface to make a 15 cm long oval.

Preheat the barbecue to a low heat. Brush the bread with a little olive oil and cook for 5 minutes, then brush the top with the remaining olive oil, flip and cook for a further 4–5 minutes until the bread is cooked through. Serve hot.

garlic bread skewers

This is a fun version of garlic bread, and the slightly smoky flavour you get from the coals is delicious. You can also add cubes of cheese such as mozzarella or fontina to the skewers.

1 baguette

150 ml extra virgin olive oil

2 garlic cloves, crushed

2 tablespoons chopped fresh parsley

sea salt and freshly ground black pepper

6–8 wooden or bamboo skewers, soaked in water before use.

SERVES 6–8

Cut the bread into 2 cm thick slices, then cut the slices crossways to make half moons.

Put the olive oil, garlic, parsley, salt and pepper into a large bowl, add the bread and toss until well coated with the parsley and oil.

Preheat the barbecue. Thread the garlic bread onto skewers and toast over medium hot coals for 2–3 minutes on each side until golden brown.

Variation

Cut 250 g mozzarella cheese into about 24 small pieces. Thread a piece of bread onto the skewer and continue to alternate the cheese and bread. Cook as in the main recipe.

sweet things

Wrapping fruits in foil is a great way to cook them on the barbecue – all the juices are contained in the parcel while the fruit softens.

grilled fruit parcels

4 peaches or nectarines, halved, stoned and sliced

200 g blueberries

125 g raspberries

freshly squeezed juice of 1 orange

1 teaspoon ground cinnamon

2 tablespoons caster sugar

200 g thick yoghurt

1 tablespoon clear honey

1 tablespoon rosewater

1 tablespoon chopped pistachio nuts, to serve

SERVES 4

Put the fruit into a large bowl, add the orange juice, cinnamon and sugar and mix well. Divide the fruit mixture evenly between 4 sheets of foil. Fold the foil over the fruit and seal the edges to make parcels.

Put the yoghurt, honey and rosewater into a separate bowl and mix well. Set aside until required.

Preheat the barbecue, then cook the parcels over medium hot coals for 5–6 minutes. Remove the parcels from the heat, open carefully and transfer to 4 serving bowls. Serve with the yoghurt and a sprinkling of pistachio nuts.

grilled figs with almond
mascarpone cream

This dish works well with stone fruits too, such as plums, peaches or nectarines.

150 g mascarpone cheese

½ teaspoon vanilla extract

1 tablespoon toasted
ground almonds

1 tablespoon Marsala wine

1 tablespoon clear honey

1 tablespoon caster sugar

1 teaspoon ground cardamom

8–10 figs, halved

SERVES 4

Put the mascarpone cheese, vanilla extract, almonds, Marsala wine and honey into a bowl and beat well. Set aside in the refrigerator until required.

Put the sugar and ground cardamom into a separate bowl and mix well. Carefully dip the cut surface of the figs into the mixture.

Preheat the barbecue, then cook the figs over medium hot coals for 1–2 minutes on each side until charred and softened.

Transfer the grilled figs to 4 serving bowls and serve with the almond mascarpone cream.

banana parcels
with chocolate and rum

4 banana leaves or aluminium foil, cut to 25 cm square

4 bananas, halved crossways

80 g dark chocolate, broken into small pieces

4 tablespoons dark rum

1 tablespoon sunflower oil (if using a pan)

whipped cream, to serve

string or raffia, soaked in water for 15 minutes

SERVES 4

Ever so slightly decadent, this dish will help you re-create the taste of the Caribbean in minutes. Equally good cooked outside on a barbecue in the heat of summer or made on a stove-top grill pan in the depths of winter.

Put the banana leaves on a work surface. On the first leaf, put 2 banana halves side by side. Sprinkle with one-quarter of the chocolate and 1 tablespoon rum. Fold up the sides and edges to form a square parcel. Tie with the wet string or raffia (soaking will prevent the string from burning). Repeat to make 4 parcels.

Put the parcels on a preheated barbecue or oiled, smoking-hot stove-top grill pan and cook for about 10 minutes on each side.

Snip the string and serve with whipped cream.

Note Banana leaves are available from larger supermarkets. To make them more malleable, put on the barbecue or grill pan for 1 minute before using. Aluminium foil makes a worthy substitute.

A simple but delicious end to a meal – the pears, blue cheese and walnuts perfectly complement one another. Serve on toast with a glass or two of dessert wine. For the best results, choose ripe but firm pears.

barbecued pears with spiced honey, walnuts and blue cheese

50 g walnuts

2 tablespoons clear honey

¼ teaspoon ground cardamom

4 pears

2 tablespoons caster sugar, for dusting

4 slices of toast

125 g Gorgonzola cheese

dessert wine, to serve

SERVES 4

Put the walnuts into a frying pan, add the honey and cardamom and cook over a high heat until the honey bubbles furiously and starts to darken. Immediately pour the mixture onto a sheet of greaseproof paper and let cool.

Peel the nuts from the paper and set aside.

Preheat the barbecue. Using a sharp knife, cut the pears into quarters and remove and discard the cores. Cut the pear quarters into thick wedges. Dust lightly with caster sugar and cook over medium hot coals for about 1½ minutes on each side.

Pile the pears onto slices of toast, sprinkle with the walnuts and crumble over some Gorgonzola cheese. Serve with a glass of dessert wine.

s'mores

16 biscuits

8 pieces of plain chocolate

16 marshmallows

8 metal skewers

SERVES 4

This is one for the kids. S'mores are an American campfire classic where graham crackers, barbecued marshmallows and chocolate squares are sandwiched together making a delicious, gooey taste sensation. Sweet biscuits, such as langue du chat or almond thins work just as well.

Put half the biscuits onto a plate and top each one with a square of chocolate.

Preheat the barbecue. Thread 2 marshmallows onto each skewer and cook over hot coals for about 2 minutes, turning constantly until the marshmallows are melted and blackened. Remove from the heat and let cool slightly.

Put the marshmallows onto the chocolate squares and sandwich together with the remaining biscuits. Gently ease out the skewers and serve the s'mores as soon as the chocolate melts.

thinly pared zest and freshly squeezed juice of 6 large unwaxed lemons

180 g sugar

sparkling water, to top up

To serve

ice cubes

fresh lemon slices

sprigs of fresh mint

SERVES 6–8

homemade fresh lemonade

Fresh lemonade is simple to make and you can keep the lemony syrup in the fridge and dilute it with either chilled sparkling water or soda water as required. You could also try adding saffron to make a golden-hued drink with an intriguing taste. Just add a pinch of saffron threads to the warm syrup when you take it off the heat.

Put the lemon zest, sugar and 600 ml of water in a saucepan and bring slowly to a simmer, stirring to dissolve the sugar. As soon as the sugar is dissolved and the syrup begins to bubble, take it off the heat. Half-cover and leave until cold.

Squeeze the lemons and add the juice to the cold syrup. Strain into a bowl, cover and chill.

Transfer the lemonade to a glass jug filled with ice cubes and add the lemon slices and mint. Dilute with sparkling water on a ratio of about 1 part syrup to 1 part water.

2 fresh peaches, stoned and thinly sliced

250 g strawberries, hulled and sliced

1 orange, sliced

150 ml crème de fraise (strawberry-flavoured liqueur)

2 x 750-ml bottles dry white wine

1 small cucumber, peeled, deseeded and thinly sliced

clear sparkling lemonade, to top up

borage flowers (optional), to serve

ice cubes, to serve

SERVES 12

peach and strawberry sangria

This is a fragrant and more delicate version of the classic Spanish sangria. You can add almost any fruit you like and vary the liqueur to your taste. Try peach schnapps or crème de framboise (raspberry-flavoured liqueur).

Put the peaches, strawberries and orange slices in a large jug with the strawberry liqueur. Pour in the wine and chill for 30 minutes. When ready to serve, add the cucumber and some ice and top up with lemonade. Pour into glasses and garnish each serving with borage flowers, if using.

cosmopolitan iced tea

30 ml vodka, vanilla-flavoured
if available

15 ml triple sec

80 ml cranberry juice

freshly squeezed juice of ½ lime

ice cubes

SERVES 1

Cranberry juice lends a light, fruity, refreshing quality
to this cocktail, where it's natural bitterness is softened
by the triple sec.

Fill a cocktail shaker with ice. Add the vodka, triple sec and
cranberry and lime juices. Replace the lid and shake briskly.
Strain into a tall glass, half-filled with ice. Serve immediately.

index

recipe credits

Ghillie Başan
char-grilled tamarind
   prawns
chicken tandoori
   kebabs
cumin-flavoured lamb
   kebabs with hot
   hoummus
curried pork satay with
   pineapple sauce
duck satay with grilled
   pineapple and plum
   sauce
fiery beef satay in
   peanut sauce
harissa chicken kebabs
   with oranges and
   preserved lemon
lamb and porcini
   kebabs with sage
   and parmesan
lamb shish kebab
   with yoghurt and
   flatbread
monkfish kebabs with
   chermoula
pork kofta kebabs with
   sweet and sour
   sauce
prawn and scallop
   kebabs with walnut
   sauce
spicy beef and coconut
   kofta kebabs
spicy chicken kebabs
   with ground almonds
spicy tofu satay with
   soy dipping sauce
stuffed char-grilled
   sardines
summer vegetable
   kebabs with
   homemade pesto
swordfish kebabs with
   oranges and sumac
vine-wrapped fish
   kebabs with tangy
   herb sauce

Fiona Beckett
Argentinian-style
   'asado' steak with
   chimichurri salsa
char-grilled steak fajitas
   with chunky
   guacamole
corn and pepper salsa
fresh tomato salsa
salsa verde

Sicilian-spiced sea
   bass with grilled
   tomatoes and baby
   fennel
Tuscan-style steak

Maxine Clark
barbecued salmon
   steaks with basil and
   parmesan butter
mustard-barbecued
   salmon tail

Ross Dobson
summer tabbouleh with
   chickpeas and spring
   salad

Jane Noraika
aubergine and smoked
   cheese rolls
banana parcels with
   chocolate and rum
plantain with lime and
   chilli

**Elsa Petersen-
Schepelern**
baba ganoush
barbecued spareribs
   with Mexican salsa
char-grilled prawns with
   avocado chilli salsa

Louise Pickford
barbecue basics text
Asian barbecue sauce
barbecue sauce
barbecued fish bathed
   in oregano and
   lemon
barbecued Mexican-
   style poussins
barbecued pears with
   spiced honey,
   walnuts and blue
   cheese
beetroot and baby
   onion brochettes
butterflied lamb with
   white bean salad
caper butter
cheeseburger
chicken lemon
   skewers
chicken kebabs
   Moroccan-style
chicken 'panini' with
   mozzarella and salsa

rossa
chicken steak burger
   with Caesar dressing
chilli cornbread
chilli jam
chunky aubergine
   burgers with pesto
clam parcels with garlic
   butter
cosmopolitan ice tea
courgette, feta and mint
   salad
creamy coleslaw
creamy corn salsa
Creole rub
duck yakitori
dukkah crusted tuna
   with preserved lemon
   salsa
ember-roasted
   potatoes
fragrant Asian rub
fragrant herb couscous
   salad
garlic bread skewers
grilled corn with chilli
   salt rub
grilled figs with almond
   mascarpone cream
grilled fruit parcels
grilled pepper butter
   sauce
grilled pita salad with
   olive salsa and
   mozzarella
grilled polenta
grilled rosemary
   flatbread
homemade fresh
   lemonade
herb butter
herb, lemon and garlic
   marinade
hot pineapple and
   papaya salsa
jerk chicken wings with
   avocado salsa
lamb burgers with mint
   yoghurt
mayonnaise
minted yoghurt
   marinade
Moroccan fish skewers
   with couscous
Moroccan rub
mushroom burgers with
   caramelized garlic
   aïoli
olive-infused chicken
   with charred lemons
open chicken burger
   with grilled
   vegetables
open Tex-Mex burger

with chilli relish
parsley, feta and pine
   nut dip
peach and strawberry
   sangria
peppered tuna steak
   with salsa rossa
piri-piri sauce
prawns with chilli oil
   and pistachio and
   mint pesto
red snapper with
   parsley salad
sage-rubbed pork
   chops
saffron butter
salad of roasted
   peppers and
   asparagus
'sausage' burgers for
   kids
seared swordfish with
   new potatoes, beans
   and olives
skewered scallops with
   coconut dressing
smoky barbecue sauce
s'mores
souvlaki with cracked
   wheat salad
spiced falafel burger
spiced pork burger with
   satay sauce
squid piri-piri
steak with blue cheese
   butter
sweet chilli sauce
Tex-Mex pork rack
Thai spice marinade
tomato, sesame and
   ginger salsa
top dogs
Vietnamese pork
   balls
whole chicken roasted
   on the barbecue
whole salmon stuffed
   with herbs

Fiona Smith
guacamole
roast garlic, paprika and
   sherry alioli
roast tomato ketchup
sweet chilli and tomato
   salsa
tomato, lemon and
   courgette relish
tzatziki

Lindy Wildsmith
barbecue basics text
aromatic pork burger in
   pitta bread

char-grilled chicken
   breast with mixed
   leaves and balsamic
   dressing
chilli tomato chutney
mango, kiwi and

coriander salsa
parsley and anchovy
   relish
peperonata
sesame sweet potato
   packets

picture credits

Martin Brigdale
Pages 4–5, 6, 9*al*, 10*bl*,
18, 37, 48, 50 inset, 51,
52, 59, 60, 64, 80, 83,
98, 101, 110, 129, 131,
163, 177, 181, 185,
188, 189, 219

Peter Cassidy
Pages 23, 27 inset, 29,
85, 90 inset, 92, 109,
117, 137, 140, 149,
155, 162, 165, 180,
208 inset, 209, 212
inset, 213, 215 inset,
221

Christopher Drake
Page 10*cl*

Daniel Farmer
Page 108

Richard Jung
Pages 3, 35, 44, 54–56,
66, 72–76, 87, 88, 96,
104*bg*, 112, 114–116,
118, 121, 125, 132
inset, 145–147, 154,
157, 161, 164, 166,
172, 174, 179, 184,
193, 195, 196, 206,
215*bg*, 230 inset, 231,
234 inset

Lisa Linder
Page 233

William Lingwood
Pages 31 inset, 138,
141, 190, 194, 224,
232, 235

Diana Miller
Pages 30, 33, 38, 39
inset, 41, 45, 136, 152,
225

David Munns
Pages 62 inset, 200

William Reavell
Pages 216, 226

Debi Treloar
Pages 7, 13, 47, 58
inset, 69, 78 inset, 104
inset, 187 inset, 191
inset

Ian Wallace
Pages 1, 2, 8, 9 *ac*, *ar*
& *b*, 10 *al*, *ar*, & *br*, 11,
12, 14, 17, 19, 21, 22,
25, 26, 34, 42, 46, 63,
67, 68, 71, 79, 84, 91,
95, 97, 102, 105–107,
113, 122, 126, 128,
130, 133, 134, 139,
142, 143 inset, 150,
153, 158, 159 inset,
160, 169–171, 173,
178, 182, 183, 186,
197, 198, 201–203,
205, 210, 211, 214,
217, 218, 220, 222,
223, 227, 228

Kate Whitaker
Pages 16, 20, 24,
27*bg*, 31*bg*, 39*bg*, 40,
43, 50*bg*, 58*bg*, 62*bg*,
70, 78*bg*, 82, 89, 90*bg*,
94, 100, 111, 119, 123,
124, 132*bg*, 135,
143*bg*, 151, 159*bg*,
168, 175, 176, 187*bg*,
191*bg*, 192, 199, 204,
208*bg*, 212*bg*, 229*bg*,
230*bg*, 234*bg*

Polly Wreford
Page 229 inset